PRAISE FOR *TOXIC FEEDBACK*

"Read this book if you are a writer in need of an insightful and compassionate guide to lead you through the mysterious terrain of literary feedback. Read this book if you are a reader who enjoys masterful storytelling in lively, accessible prose. *Toxic Feedback* is more than a manual for writers; it is itself a teacher, a friend, and an enjoyable, enlightening narrative experience. Joni Cole's voice is rich and full and accompanied by a chorus of leading writers from all walks of life sharing wisdom they have gleaned from their personal and (often hilarious) literary journeys. *Toxic Feedback* is an invitation to join the conversation no matter where you are in your own writing life."
—Emily Bernard, author of *Black Is the Body: Stories from My Grandmother's Time, My Mother's Time, and Mine*

"There are so many uninteresting and unusable books on how to write, but Joni Cole's isn't one of them. She cuts to the chase of what it means to write well, and to edit yourself with the kind of rigor that's necessary to make your work what it needs to be successful."
—Jervey Tervalon, author, lecturer in creative writing at UC–Santa Barbara, and founder of LitFest Pasadena

"Gentle reader, sensitive writer, you have found the writing guide you're looking for. Joni Cole's *Toxic Feedback* provides just what you need not only to survive but to thrive in the lonely writing life, an intimidating workshop, a competitive MFA program, or the difficult publishing market. Here you will learn how to

receive tough feedback, ignore unproductive comments, develop a supportive community, and become the writer you want to be. With useful tips and hilarious stories, Cole shows you how to be the 'boss of your own story' and take creative control of your writing life. Instead of dwelling on rejections and disappointments, she urges us to take what's useful about feedback and leave what's not—including self-doubt—behind. Above my desk, I'm putting Joni Cole's advice: 'Write more, write better, be happier.'"
—Camille Guthrie, author of *Diamonds: Poems*

"Decades ago, I asked family and friends to critique my short stories. I thought saying, 'I want you to be brutally honest' showed an element of courage, but, alas, my ego was crushed. *Toxic Feedback* helped me become a more responsible writer by accepting that criticism was not a knock against me, but rather a way to help determine whether my writing reached readers effectively. I love this book!"
—Michael Skinner, columnist for the *Courier-Gazette* of Rockland, Maine

"Step-by-step, *Toxic Feedback* guides writers—new and experienced—through what creative writing feedback is, why it so often goes so wrong, and how we can get it right. *Toxic Feedback* also beautifully and clearly shares stories and interviews about feedback. In the end, we readers learn so much about the power of feedback and how to use it to propel us toward powerful writing lives."
—Sean Prentiss, author of *Advanced Creative Nonfiction*

"Joni B. Cole's *Toxic Feedback* is a revelation of writerly affirmation! It's a jubilant celebration for those who toil over the written word! Throughout these essays and interviews, Cole reminds us that the crafting, sharing, and discussing of our words can—and should—be joyful. In a world where writers so often hear 'It's all wrong,' *Toxic Feedback* insists on building up instead of tearing down."
—Steven Coughlin, author of *Deep Cuts*

"Providing feedback is a constructive skill that needs to be nurtured. Cole's book gets to the heart of the underlying human nature of how people absorb feedback. Its lessons apply to teachers, supervisors, coaches ... anyone in a position of power."—Rebecca Joffrey, digital strategist, Cornell University

"Cole's writing sparkles with humor and honesty.... [Cole] shows that the power of positive feedback is amazing.... *Toxic Feedback* makes me crave the kinds of responses that will expand my mind and make me productive."
—*Writer Advice*

"Cole's book is certainly needed; the feedback process merits far more attention than it usually receives."
—*The Writer Magazine*

"[Cole] reminds me of some of my favorite writing authorities—Natalie Goldberg, Anne Lamott, and, of course, Stephen King. And as these accomplished authors do, Cole actually imparts useful wisdom, not just on finding and understanding feedback, but on the general process of writing."
—*Blogcritics.org*

"Best for writers of fiction and creative nonfiction, great for editors and workshop leaders, and certainly an interesting read for other sorts of writers, this book is a strong addition to any writer's bookshelf."
—*Freelance-zone.com*

"Strongly recommended for academic libraries and public libraries supporting writers."
—*Library Journal*

TOXIC FEEDBACK

JONI B. COLE

Helping Writers Survive and Thrive

Revised and Expanded Edition

UNIVERSITY OF NEW MEXICO PRESS   ALBUQUERQUE

University of New Mexico Press Edition © 2023 by Joni B. Cole
All rights reserved. Published 2023
Printed in the United States of America

ISBN 978-0-8263-6483-8 (paper)
ISBN 978-0-8263-6484-5 (electronic)

Library of Congress Cataloging-in-Publication data is on file
with the Library of Congress.

Founded in 1889, the University of New Mexico sits on the
traditional homelands of the Pueblo of Sandia. The original
peoples of New Mexico—Pueblo, Navajo, and Apache—since
time immemorial have deep connections to the land and have
made significant contributions to the broader community
statewide. We honor the land itself and those who remain
stewards of this land throughout the generations and also
acknowledge our committed relationship to Indigenous peoples.
We gratefully recognize our history.

Cover and interior design by Isaac Morris
Composed in Gil Sans and Garamond Premier
Illustrations by Helmut Baer

Note: Some names of individuals and identifying features of
stories in this book have been changed to maintain privacy.

CONTENTS

Giving Feedback

In the Company of Writers

In from the Cold

When the University of New Mexico Press invited me to create a second edition of *Toxic Feedback,* originally published in 2006, my first reaction was—*I wrote that book when? I must have been in first grade!* Now that I think about it, even when I was in first grade, feedback—though I didn't know the word at the time—was already shaping my writing life. I recall my teacher, Mrs. Mundorf, and her approval of my use of capital letters . . . along with her disapproval of my abundance of exclamation points. So sowed the seeds of two of the most important things I believe writers need to understand about feedback: positive responses to our work can be both instructional and motivating, and we don't have to act on every suggestion that comes our way, even if it's from a teacher!!!

It is a gift to revisit a previously published book with the opportunity for a do-over. What still resonates? How has my perspective on the feedback interaction shifted or broadened in the interim between editions? What more needs to be shared about this delicate dynamic between reader and responder? Seventeen years is a long shelf life for an academic book, and a lot of things can change.

Indeed, several things have changed. For starters, since the original release of *Toxic Feedback,* I have worked with thousands of aspiring and seasoned authors who take my in-person and online classes through my own writer's center in Vermont as well as at conferences and writing programs around the country. It still startles me how much I continue to appreciate and learn from these story discussions across genres. It still inspires me to be in the company of working writers, bearing witness as they develop, strengthen, and polish their prose, much of their progress informed by feedback.

Another change that happened after the initial release of *Toxic Feedback* is that I published a second writing guide. That book, *Good Naked: How to Write More, Write Better, and Be Happier,* reflects my valiant attempt to bust open the myth of the suffering artist. Of course writing can be hard at times; there's no news there. But *Good Naked* illuminates the many ways newbies and seasoned authors can cultivate a productive and positive creative process every draft of the way. Oh—and back to this book—one of those ways is to seek feedback and forge connections with your fellow writers.

So yes, my professional life has evolved, and I like to think I have evolved with it, despite my reluctance to update my author photo. What hasn't changed, however, is my conviction that feedback in its many iterations plays a vital role in our creative lives. Often, feedback is the difference between writing and not writing. It can also be the difference between writing and writing well. Yet too many aspiring authors avoid or mismanage this invaluable resource for reasons that may be totally understandable but are nevertheless whacked.

I'm terrified of getting feedback. What if everybody hates my writing?

I never share my drafts. The last thing I need is someone messing with my story.

The only kind of feedback that matters is brutal honesty.

My goal in the second edition of this book—enhanced with several new chapters, author interviews, and comic illustrations—is to continue to pop these misguided thought bubbles. Yes, getting many things—kidney stones, an audit from the IRS, a creepy clown doll from a secret admirer—can be terrifying, but feedback does not have to be one of them. Yes, there are times it benefits your creative process to avoid outside opinions, but there are just as many times when feedback in one of its myriad forms can enlighten and animate your work. And no, brutal honesty is not the ultimate objective when seeking or giving feedback, unless your definition of "ultimate" is "savagely violent."

From my ongoing experience as a writer, teacher, and human being, I would say toxic feedback remains endemic in the writing world, and that includes all the ways we trash talk our own work. But I also know that feedback—when thoughtfully offered and received—is one of the most effective ways not only to survive but to thrive in our writing lives.

I think it bears noting here one other change in recent years, which makes our attention to the feedback interaction all the more important. Blame it on the proliferation of fake news, or *Game of Thrones,* or all that blue light emanating from our devices and disrupting our sleep patterns, but the level of civility in our world seems to have taken a nosedive. Politicians berate and taunt their colleagues across the aisle like schoolyard bullies. Every day we hear stories of airline passengers so ill-behaved it would be preferable to be seated next to a real screaming baby. At work, online, in city traffic, and on small-town bleachers, it feels like there's a new kind of contagion in the air, its symptoms fluctuating from rudeness to rage.

I like to think I have outgrown my own screaming-baby tendencies, but, alas, I am equally susceptible to bad behavior. Recently I got a call from the nice woman who works at the heating and plumbing company, telling me that she needed to reschedule my appointment to fix a faulty thermostat.

"I'm so sorry," she said, "but our technician got called out to an emergency." She added something about another customer's furnace breaking down and how the family had no heat. This was January in Vermont, with temperatures below freezing. My own heating system was working just fine, notwithstanding a faulty thermostat.

"But my appointment was scheduled weeks ago," I reminded her.

"Is your situation also an emergency?" the lady asked, concern in her voice. "I could try to reroute another technician, but they're all out straight."

"No, it's not an emergency," I snapped, "but I stayed home from work just so I could be here for the appointment." (This was a lie. I work from home.)

"I'm so sorry," the lady from the company repeated. "I know this is inconvenient."

"Let me speak to your manager!" Actually, I didn't say that last part, thank goodness, but I did think it, which still makes me that kind of person in my head.

Later, as I reflected on this exchange in the warmth of my well-heated condo, I was taken aback by my obnoxious behavior, my lack of perspective, my absence of common, human decency. Good grief, I thought, those other people had a broken furnace. In January. In Vermont. Pipes could have frozen! A family could have died!

I am not going to pretend that I, or this book, can fully reverse the decline of civility. Clearly I have my own work to do when interacting with people in the world at large. But in the writing realm, I do believe the insights offered on these pages can help all of us demystify and detoxify the feedback interaction—and change our writing lives for the better. Both giving and receiving feedback takes skill and heart. At its most effective, feedback is a form of communication grounded not just in civility but in thoughtfulness, mutual respect, even loving-kindness.

I know associating feedback with loving-kindness may sound shocking. Almost as shocking as someone complaining about a canceled appointment because her service technician needed to save another family from hypothermia. In a feedback interaction, the stakes may not be quite so life and death, but they can feel that way given how much our writing matters to us, how important it is to get it right. I may still be living with a faulty thermostat ("What do you mean your next available appointment isn't for three weeks?!"), but even I don't think any writer should be left out in the cold.

Every Writer Has a Story

Back when my former husband was in graduate school and I was still trying to figure out what to do with my life, I decided to take a continuing education course in fiction writing. My professor had all the markings of a genius, literary and otherwise. His novels broke ground and enjoyed dismal sales. Like so many writers from Lord Byron to Joyce Carol Oates, he assigned a fascination to the sport of boxing that is lost on me. And his course cost $2,432, an amount roughly equivalent to the annual earnings of a freelance writer, which I happened to be at the time.

Once a week, every student submitted a story to the professor, who then judged whether it was worthy of discussion by the group. If he chose your story for the class to discuss that evening, he insisted the writer remain anonymous, similar to how news organizations handle the coverage of crimes committed by juvenile delinquents. With great trepidation, I submitted my first piece to the professor. Because my entire self-worth (back then, anyway) depended on the professor's reaction to those eleven pages, I cheated, naturally. I submitted a story I had been working on diligently for over a year. This was a story excavated from the mines of my personality, roiling in turmoil yet tinged with bittersweet humor. This was a story forged in the traditional framework of conflict, crisis, epiphany, resolution. This was a story I had received an A on in a community college creative-writing class I had participated in a few months earlier.

This was *not* the story the professor chose for discussion. That evening, our class critiqued a short piece that consisted entirely of messages on a suicidal woman's answering machine. In hindsight, I realize that this was the more sophisticated story, actually quite powerful, but that's not the point of this anecdote.

After class, the professor summoned me and the other writer-rejects to his podium and wordlessly returned our submissions from the previous week. The teacher's stigmata of academia—the shapeless brown corduroy blazer with blue slacks, the faint odor of a tobacco shop from the 1960s, the world-weary weight of his briefcase—all precluded me from wasting his time by asking, "Well?" Later, however, behind the lowered, green industrial shades that accessorized my apartment in married student housing, I extracted the manuscript from my backpack and searched the story page by page for his feedback.

Nothing. Nada. No red ink, no finger smudges, no telltale splotches of bourbon. Then I turned the manuscript over and there, on the back of the back page, I found it. The professor's feedback, three scrawled words: "It's all wrong." That was the professor's response to a year's worth of creative effort. *It's all wrong.* What was I to do with that? Outside my drawn shades, I could hear the barely muted roar of the university's lawn-care crew racing around on their riding mowers, charged with keeping the grounds of married student housing as close-cropped as Forrest Gump's head. Rrrr. *It's all wrong.* Rrrr. *It's all wrong.* To this day, whenever I hear the roar of a riding mower, the phrase "It's all wrong" reverberates between my ears.

Later, I calculated the cost of that professor's feedback: $810 per word, based on the class tuition. But his feedback cost me much more than money. Those three words confirmed what my own insecurities had been whispering to me all along: *I was an outsider; I had nothing of importance to say; I would never be a real writer.* The professor's response to my writing is what I call "toxic feedback." It made me lose ground and lose confidence as a writer.

That fiction-writing class is ancient history, but my experience with toxic feedback left an indelible impression on my psyche. I almost quit writing; but I didn't. I went on to become an author, supplemented by other labels over the years: teacher, editor, speaker, and office temp worker, not necessarily in that order. Despite the professor's blow to my self-esteem (he never did choose any of my work for discussion during the class), I continued to write because writing for me, as is the case with so many people, isn't simply a matter of confidence or success, but compulsion.

Something inside writers makes them need to put words on the page, regardless of the risk to their tender egos. Writers may ignore or deny that need for years out of fear or with good excuses or lame excuses, but the need remains, manifesting in a sense of excitement and agitation whenever an intriguing idea or character pops into their consciousness, whispering insistently, *"Write about me! Write about me! Wouldn't I make a great story?!"* You know this anticipatory, antsy feeling if you are a writer. You also know this feeling if you have ever taken Dayquil.

For so many years I have stopped counting, I have been teaching creative writing to adults in my community and around the globe, thanks to Zoom. Some of the participants who come to my writing workshops are new to the craft, while others have been publishing for years. Some join the group because they are in the throes of working on their latest novel or a memoir; others join because they need help getting started. Some have never been in a creative writing workshop. Others have already earned MFAs. Regardless of these differences, most of them arrive at that first meeting ready to bolt. As the participants introduce themselves to the other members in the workshop, they begin to apron-wring and apologize for their narrative failures before they have even shared one word of their work in class. They admit they are nervous wrecks about submitting their stories to the group for feedback. Where is this coming from? These people are not wimps. By day, they take on much riskier tasks: brain surgery, child-rearing, insurance billing. So why would a writing workshop intimidate them? Of course, I knew the answer all along.

It's all wrong.

Almost every writer has a story, some sad tale about how a teacher, critique group or workshop, friend, boss, spouse, parent, agent, editor, or rogue reader provided them with toxic feedback that made them doubt their abilities, distrust their own voices, sabotage their stories, or just feel really, really lousy. Once exposed to toxic feedback, some people stop writing, sometimes for years, sometimes for a lifetime. Others keep scribbling away but avoid feedback for fear of harsh criticism, burying their unread novels or poems or essays at the bottom of their sock drawers, alongside other shameful secrets like those leftover European Royalty diet capsules and miracle wrinkle removers ordered after seeing some Facebook ad. Still others continue to write and solicit feedback, viewing the process as a necessary evil.

Necessary it is. Evil, it isn't—because only feedback can answer the ultimate question: Are you connecting with your readers? With the exception of creating a secret diary or a grocery list, most writing is intended to communicate something meaningful to a person other than yourself, whether it is a life story shared in a personal essay or the power of forgiveness in a ten-line verse. Without the benefit of feedback during the drafting process, how do you know whether your words are achieving your intent? How do you recognize the weak passages or missed opportunities when your only perspective is the one inside your own head? How do you know if the reader is moved by your writing or wants to move on?

The time has come to rid the world of toxic feedback so that writers can avail themselves of this invaluable but too often tainted resource. With the understanding that it takes two to create toxic feedback, we can move beyond pseudo-solutions for improving the feedback process, such as simply telling writers to toughen up, as if toxic feedback would not be an issue if these artistic types would just get a backbone. We can also stop vilifying feedback providers, as if their lack of awareness of what motivates and instructs writers makes them inherently toxic. I suppose there are a few feedback providers who are truly malevolent, but my experience in countless interactions has made me realize that most people who comment on our work mean well, even when they are saying something horrifically insensitive. Even people in love, *especially* people in love, generate toxic feedback. Consider the true story of the once happily married writers who provided feedback to each other during their collaboration on a self-help book. The book was successful, but now the children only see their father every other weekend.

The intent of *Toxic Feedback* is to help aspiring authors not only survive criticism but thrive in the feedback process. This book is for every struggling writer who wants to do less struggling and more writing. (Can you imagine!) It is for feedback providers who want to empower writers and enjoy the sense of satisfaction that comes from helping someone achieve a work of merit. And it is for writing workshops and critique groups that want to leave every participant informed and energized by this communal experience.

My own experiences receiving and giving feedback contributed to the insights and opinions that follow, as did my conversations with a diversity of writers, teachers, editors, and other knowledgeable people inside and outside the writing realm. This book also includes my interviews with an array of successful authors across genres, who generously shared their own feedback stories from the inspiring to the deranged.

Despite all the evidence to the contrary, the myth of the lone (and lonely) writer continues to loom large, and with it the unhealthy assumption that "real" writers toil in isolation. By offering instruction to writers and feedback providers on how to manage this vital but delicate dynamic, my hope is to dispel this myth once and for all. Yes, writing is a solitary effort, but it doesn't have to be a lonely one—and that is the real gift of feedback.

4

"Do you think it was the positive feedback?"

WHAT IS FEEDBACK?

It seemed like a good idea to start this book with an official definition of the term *feedback*. So I consulted some online dictionaries, and here is what I found.

I found the definition of feedback as it relates to cybernetics and control theory. I found how the term is used in electronic and mechanical engineering, economics and finance, gaming, organizations, biology, and nature. I found diagrams of feedback loops with lots of arrows pointing here and there. I found exotic-looking translations of the word (*terugkoppeling*... *Rückkopplung* ... αυἀδραση ...). But what I didn't find was a definition for feedback as it specifically relates to writing.

How can this be? I knew writers had co-opted the term from some other realm (electrical engineering, as it turns out, circa 1920, according to the *Oxford English Dictionary*), but you would think that by now our application of *feedback* would have merited its own place in the dictionary, especially since we use the term all the time. "I joined a writing group because I want feedback." "I'm waiting for feedback from my editor." "Winston wants me to give him feedback on his story, but I don't have a clue what to say to him."

So with no dictionary definition to help us out, what exactly are we all talking about when we talk about feedback?

I think a lot of writers view feedback as someone telling them what's wrong with their writing in order to help them fix it. That may be one way to think of feedback, but it sure doesn't make me want to race out and get some. As a writer, just the thought of readers focusing on my imperfections takes me back to the junior prom, with everyone staring at the zit on my nose, but no one even noticing my pretty pink dress. And, as a feedback provider, the responsibility of helping writers "fix" their stories only makes me feel desperate to find fault with them, even where there is none.

It seems to me that as writers and feedback providers we need to change the way most of us perceive feedback. We need to come up with our own definition of the term, one that distinguishes it entirely from feedback as it applies to electrical engineering, for example, with its dry references to input and output, and its awful association with that shrieking sound coming from the PA system. We need to put a positive spin on feedback as it relates to writing, and we need to do it quickly before it's too late for damage control. Otherwise, the term *feedback* is in real danger of going the way of *criticism,* a word once connoting praise as well as censure but that is now just a big, fat negative in most people's minds.

We can't let that happen to feedback. We just can't. Because the essence of feedback is nothing but positive (even when it is negative), and we are only hurting ourselves if we overlook its real meaning and value.

For a writer, feedback means you never have to write in a vacuum. It means that whenever you need or crave a connection to a real live reader, there it is, yours for the asking. And the beauty of feedback is—you can take it or leave it! Part of the reason we shy away from feedback is because we assign it the power of a mandate or a judgment. Feedback is neither of those things. It is simply a resource to help you create the poems or stories or essays you want to create; to help you be the writer you want to be.

Consider all the ways that feedback can serve you in achieving your goals. Feedback can help you polish your skills, hone your writerly instincts, and massage your words into shapely prose or poetry much faster than going it alone. Equally important, feedback can serve as a source of inspiration and motivation. It can energize you to go at it again, make it better, dig deeper, and discover for yourself what happens next and why. Creating an inspired and polished work can be a long and murky process. No wonder so many writers are plagued by two debilitating questions: What the hell am I trying to say here? And who the hell cares anyway? Feedback is one of the best defenses against this kind of self-doubt and its parasitic sidekick, writer's block.

Writers need to come up with a definition of feedback that embraces all of these positive attributes. And while we are at it, we need to make sure that our definition takes into account the fact that feedback can manifest in a multitude of forms. Yes, feedback can be a critical response to a manuscript, someone telling the writer what is wrong with his writing. That may be exactly the form of feedback that serves the writer best, depending on where the story is at and where the writer's head is at on any given day.

But feedback can also take the form of listening to a writer talk about his work. "Wow, tell me more about this sculptor in twelfth-century France." "Tell me why it matters to this old woman to live out her life in her own home."

"Tell me how this chess fanatic uses the game to avoid the reality of his bad marriage." Letting the writer hear herself talk—and showing that you are interested in her subject matter—not only helps her crystallize her thoughts but also helps to solidify her faith in the project.

Feedback can take the form of brainstorming. "What if you gave your narrator a secret crush?" "What if you set the story in an Alaskan village rather than downtown Seattle?" "What if you moved these seven paragraphs around?" This form of feedback stimulates the writer's creativity, reminding him that the story's elements are hers to manipulate and recreate as she sees fit.

Feedback can be an affirmation. "You're doing great!" "I know you can do this!" "I can't wait to read more!"

Feedback can be a kick in the pants. "I want to see a second draft by next Thursday at 4:00."

Or feedback can simply be a walk around the block with a friend, because sometimes what you need more than anything is to get away from writing for a spell. Your conversation doesn't even have to be about the story, because while you and your friend are debating whether you would want your dogs cloned or complaining about those neighbors who let their kids run wild, your right brain will be doing its thing, quietly making connections, registering patterns, and solving your plot snarl for you.

So what is the definition of feedback as it relates to writing? Given all the positive things that feedback can help achieve, and all the useful forms that feedback can take, I would define feedback as *any response* to writers or their work that helps them write more and write better. Better yet, I would define feedback as any response that helps writers write more, write better, and be happier (because writers are always happier when they are writing successfully).

Now *that* is the kind of definition that would put a positive spin on feedback. That is the kind of definition that would encourage even the most skittish writers to avail themselves of this terrific resource throughout the creative process. In fact, that is the perfect definition of feedback as it relates to writing, or at least the perfect definition according to me. And because you won't find a better one anywhere in the dictionary, let's all consider mine as the definitive meaning of the word.

feed•back \ fēd-bak (*noun, often attributive*): any response to writers or their work that helps them write more, write better, and be happier.

Doesn't a definition like that make you want to race out and get some?

EQ

People are not supposed to know their IQs. Schools, for example, go to great lengths to hide IQ scores from students and their parents, locking the records in remote file cabinets where only the guidance counselor and the janitor can access them when necessary. I can tell you from personal experience that this policy of secrecy should never be lifted.

I know my IQ, and this knowledge has caused me nothing but grief. My former husband, unfortunately for him, is to blame. Steve is a clinical psychologist, and when we got married he was still in graduate school. Part of his training meant learning how to give IQ tests, so one day I agreed he could practice on me. Big mistake. In retrospect, it's obvious that no couple should engage in this kind of behavior, because there is some information—how you eat when no one is looking, the number of your former sex partners, and exactly how smart you really are (versus how smart you *think* you are)—that should remain outside the bounds of marital knowledge. Still, I was a starry-eyed newlywed at the time and wanted to help out my beloved. I also was sure I could nail that IQ test to the wall.

As part of the test, Steve read off a long span of digits and made me recite them backward from memory. He showed me pictures that I had to arrange in a logical sequence. He asked me if I knew the name of the president during the Civil War. Up to this point in the testing I was doing great, imagining my IQ right up there alongside those of Albert Einstein, and Hedy Lamarr, and whoever the genius was who figured out you could eat a pineapple.

Then came object assembly, a test of spatial reasoning. My hubby handed me some puzzle pieces, told me to fit them together into a recognizable object, and started his stopwatch. I turned the pieces this way and that, assembling them in all sorts of permutations. Were they supposed to form an elephant? A tree? An elephant stuck in a tree? As the minutes ticked away, so did the points of my IQ. My husband finally had to pry the still-disjointed pieces out of my hands. From there, things went downhill fast.

After the testing, Steve combined all the subtest scores, scaled everything in accordance with my age, and calculated my full-scale IQ. He was reluctant to tell me the number until I threatened to adopt one of those Vietnamese pigs for a pet, which happened to be all the rage at the time. I wish he had opted for the pig.

For years I suffered within the confines of my limited IQ. Like most people, I was conditioned to believe that intellectual intelligence is the best measure of human potential. As a result, I went through my young adulthood convinced I was doomed to only a slightly above-average future. Then, in the early 1990s, came a burst of good news. Two psychologists named John Mayer and Peter Salovey introduced the concept of EQ in the *Journal of Personality Assessment*. In case you missed that issue, *EQ* stands for Emotional Intelligence Quotient, and it is an alternative way to assess intelligence. Like your IQ, your EQ is also a predictor of future success, only instead of assessing your intellectual abilities, your EQ measures your emotional intelligence—how good you are at acting appropriately, based on your understanding of your own emotions and the emotions of others. A high EQ indicates you are likely to perform well at school, at home, and on the job. A low EQ means you might want to stick to something like making pottery or computer programming.

Well, as soon as I heard the news about EQ, I knew I had to know mine. For this testing, though, I was determined to get a more professional assessment, so I filled out an EQ questionnaire in a woman's magazine. That is how I discovered that my EQ ran circles around my IQ. Suddenly I realized that I had just as much potential as all those brainiacs with higher IQs. In fact, I actually had *more* potential because, when it comes to success, EQ matters even more than IQ, at least according to some experts. Armed with this new insight, my approach to life changed forever and my future never looked brighter.

There is nothing like a fresh perspective.

The time has come for a fresh perspective on the feedback process, as well—one that takes into account not only the intellectual factors that support good writing and critiquing but the emotional factors that also play a crucial role in the feedback process. "Emotions?" You ask. "What do they have to do with addressing weak characterizations, thin plots, and passive verb choices?" "Everything," I say, because if both the writer and the feedback provider are unaware of their own and the other person's needs, feelings, and motives, then the feedback process is likely to do more harm than good.

Consider a typical feedback scenario. On one side of the feedback process is the writer; and, let's face it, every writer is a basket case. Yet, like Tolstoy's unhappy families, every writer is a basket case in her own way, which is why one writer may find a particular comment helpful, while another writer may be crushed by the exact same comment and do something drastic, like chuck writing altogether and subscribe to all two hundred streaming services. On the other side of the exchange is the feedback provider. This person's first concern, naturally, is to sound smart, which is why so many workshop peers and writing instructors often end up trouncing around the submitter's psyche like Thing One and Thing Two in *The Cat in the Hat*, not intending to harm but generating a lot of toxic feedback nonetheless.

I remember being in a workshop years ago with a twenty-something woman who felt compelled to tell an older writer in the group that her memoir about growing up on a small farm wasn't "meaningful." Trying to be helpful, the twenty-something advised the woman to write about the child-welfare system or overcrowded prisons, something that actually had significance. Not surprisingly, this feedback provider went on to become a social worker. She is a good person. But her feedback was toxic, causing the writer to doubt the value of her own existence.

In my roles as workshop leader and editor, I, too, have made plenty of toxic bloopers. Maybe I said too much or too little. Maybe I worried more about what I had to say than what the writer needed to hear. Maybe I was just having a bad hair day and was distracted by the fact that my head had suddenly sprouted a hay bale. Regardless of the specifics, in each of these situations I must have left my EQ in my other purse, because the result of my feedback was that the writer ended up feeling overwhelmed or despondent or wanted me to spontaneously combust. It doesn't get much more toxic than that.

For both writers and feedback providers, applying emotional intelligence is the key to detoxifying the feedback process. Writers, if you want to use feedback to be a better, more productive writer, you need to pay attention to your feelings. What kind of feedback motivates you? What causes you to melt down? At what stage in the writing process do you often feel stuck? How can you manage the feedback process in a way that feels supportive and productive? How are you getting in your own way when processing feedback?

Feedback providers, you need to be equally attuned to the emotional components of the process. What is your personal agenda? What impact are your words having on the writer? Are you paying attention to what the writer really needs to hear, right at that moment, to move their work forward? When writers entrust us with their works in progress, it is our responsibility to remember that there is an actual living, breathing, sentient person on the other end of our responses.

Let me add here, in case you think I have gone off the touchy-feely deep end, that communication experts far more clinically minded than I'll ever be have weighed the relevance of emotion in the feedback process. As a result, we now have formulas such as the "feedback sandwich," which advises that when you are critiquing something—whether it is an employee's job performance or a writer's manuscript—you will meet with more receptivity if you start with a positive comment and end with a positive comment, sandwiching the downer comment in the middle. Other communication experts go even farther, advocating for a four-to-one ratio of positive to negative (or "kiss to kick") comments.

Goodness knows, all those feeding frenzies that pass as writing workshops would be well served if only there were some kind of formula to stop the madness. But formulas for doling out positives and negatives don't always help, especially since those terms can often be confusing. Here is what I mean. Most people think positive feedback is when a reader says something nice about a writer's story, and negative feedback is when the reader says something critical. An example of positive feedback might be, "Gee, you write just like Stephen King." An example of negative feedback might be, "Gee, you write just like Stephen King." Do you see the difference? Neither do I.

To address the problem of toxic feedback, we need to remember that feedback isn't simply an equation that can be solved with formulas and ratios; rather, it is an *interaction* between humans, one in which personality and temperament (not to mention alcohol, Adderall, and chocolate) all have a significant effect on the outcome. Overlook the human factor during the feedback interaction, and you are ignoring the heart that gives writing its life.

As writers and feedback providers, one of the smartest things we can do is to be conscious of the emotional factors that inspire or undermine the creative process. Whether we are on the giving or receiving end of feedback, success comes from understanding our own feelings and the feelings of others and acting accordingly. Maybe potters and computer programmers can function in their work just fine without emotional intelligence, but when the work involves humans, it's a different story. After all, it doesn't take an Einstein to figure out that humans are nothing if not emotional.

SARAH STEWART TAYLOR:
"WOW! THIS COULD BE MY JOB."

When mystery novelist Sarah Stewart Taylor (author of the acclaimed Maggie D'arcy series) was in ninth grade, her English teacher, Mrs. Mongoluzzi, gave the class an assignment: take a Robert Frost poem and write a piece of fiction about it. Sarah chose "Fire and Ice," a nine-line verse that ponders how the world will end. Sarah created a story that took place after a nuclear holocaust, about a lone woman with her baby wandering across the apocalyptic landscape describing what happened. "From what I remember," says Sarah, "there's this revelation at the end of the story that survival is futile. A classic freshman mentality," she laughs.

Sarah also remembers that this was one of the first assignments that didn't feel like an assignment. "I wasn't thinking about how long it would take me. I was really on fire when I was writing" (no pun intended). A few days after Sarah turned in the assignment, Mrs. Mongoluzzi asked her to stay after class. The teacher walked Sarah out into the hallway. "I can still see her," Sarah says, "very elegant, very Talbot's. A formal person, but she loved literature. She told me, 'You know, *you're a writer.*' It was one of those really powerful moments. I remember so vividly standing in the hall of that high school and having this feeling of joy. I remember thinking, *Wow! This could be my job.*"

Sarah had a comparable defining moment at age twenty-two during a creative-writing class at Trinity College in Dublin. She'd gone to graduate school to study literature, thinking she would be an academic, but she still sought out writing classes, hoping for encouragement. At Trinity her instructor was Thomas Kilroy, best known as a playwright but also an award-winning novelist once short-listed for the Booker Prize. The class had been discussing

Sarah's work, many of the students projecting their own styles onto her writing. "There was this guy writing a Faulknerian short story complaining I wasn't Faulknerian enough," Sarah recalls. "The sci-fi writer wanted more aliens. I remember near the end of the discussion, the instructor said, 'I'm not going to say I agree or disagree, but I am going to say that Sarah should just keep writing this novel and try to get it published.'"

After graduation Sarah worked as a newspaper reporter and editor, an assistant to a literary agent, a teacher in a prison, and a community-college professor. While working these jobs she also labored for several years on a mystery novel, featuring amateur detective and art historian Sweeney St. George, who specializes in gravestones and funerary art. Published in 2003, that novel, *O'Artful Death,* earned her an Agatha Award nomination and spawned three more Sweeney mysteries.

O'Artful Death was similar to the novel Sarah presented to her creative-writing class at Trinity only in the fact that both stories were set in a Vermont arts colony. But the two books—one published, one long abandoned—are forged by a deeper connection.

"Basically, what Tom was saying in front of that writing class was, 'Don't listen to them.' He was saying, 'You can.' It was that same feeling of joy I had in ninth grade," Sarah recalls. "It was such a small thing what he said—'I think you should try to publish this.' He may have said it to twenty other students that term, but it hit some nerve. I remember walking home after class that day. I lived in this part of Dublin called Irishtown, and it was a long walk along the docks. I remember it vividly, this feeling of wanting to skip down the docks."

"Aren't you supposed to love everything I write?"

IS IT YOU . . . OR IS IT THEM?

When a feedback provider criticizes a writer's work—say he tells the writer his story could use some editing, or it is pretty clever, or he didn't get around to reading it yet—a lot of writers react in one of the following ways. They either begin loathing themselves because they are obviously terrible writers, or they begin loathing the feedback provider because he is clearly mean and insensitive or knows nothing about being an artist. If you are a writer yourself, you are likely to think these responses to feedback are perfectly normal. If you are a mentally secure individual, you are likely to recognize these reactions as *over*reactions that could be counterproductive when trying to write more and write better.

As a writer, you have no hope of surviving, let alone thriving in, the feedback process if you don't first recognize your own role in creating the kind of toxicity that can result in literary paralysis or shooting yourself in the foot. Therefore, if either of these overreactions mirrors your typical response to feedback, here is a suggestion. The next time you find yourself immediately feeling angry or defensive or despondent during a critique of your work, ask yourself the following question: Is it you . . . or is it them? Think about this seriously. Dig deep in your soul for a second or two. Soon the answer will be obvious. It is you, of course. You. You. You. Definitely you.

Yes, you.

In fact, even when it is them, it is still also you because, when it comes to hearing feedback, most writers are chasms of hypersensitivity. At the mere whiff of a critical remark we lose any sense of perspective, not to mention humor. Chalk this up to our artistic temperaments, or maybe some atavistic fight-or-flight response left over from our cave-writing days. Regardless, the truth remains the same. When it comes to our prose or poetry, we are predisposed to overreacting to feedback, a characteristic as indicative of our status as writers as hemophilia is evidence of royal lineage in Russia.

Despite this reality, some writers profess to be perfectly secure in their abilities to respond rationally to criticism. To prove their point, these "secure" writers aggressively solicit negative feedback. "Tell it to me straight," they say to their fellow workshop participants or editors or spouses. "I want you to be brutally honest." When I hear someone say words to this effect, a big alarm goes off in my head. *Code H! Code H! This is an especially hypersensitive person!*

For this insight, I have Jim to thank, a pharmacist and gifted writer who took one of my first fiction-writing workshops. When Jim introduced himself to the group, he announced that he had been writing stories for years. He had shared his work with family and friends, and they had all praised his efforts, but these were *nice* people—Jim dismissed them with a wave of his nail-gnawed hand. What he wanted from me and the other workshop members was *serious* feedback. To drive home the point that he could handle tough criticism, Jim also let us know that he was training for a marathon and restored vintage Mustangs.

Eager for this serious feedback, Jim was the first workshop participant to submit a manuscript for discussion. The piece was a short story about a character who, coincidentally, restored vintage Mustangs and was training for a marathon. Already, Jim had demonstrated his grasp of one of the most popular, albeit limiting, tenets of storytelling: write what you know.

The following week, the group discussed Jim's fiction. The readers were generous in their admiration, and the tone of the discussion was upbeat. As usual when a good story launches the workshop, some of the other participants started issuing warnings about how their own future submissions were sure to pale in comparison. This, too, had to make Jim feel good.

A few days after the meeting, my phone rang late in the evening. The good news was that the late call did not mark the demise of a relative. The bad news was that the caller was a devastated Jim, who told me that he was going to drop out of the workshop. Clearly everyone in the group had hated his story. He had decided to quit writing and focus solely on doling out pharmaceuticals, a far more rewarding pursuit even in this age of Medigap. After about an hour on the phone, I managed to convince Jim to continue attending the workshop. He agreed, reluctantly, though it was clear he still had some doubts.

Was it me . . . or was it Jim?

My take on the discussion of Jim's story was that the other workshop members had clearly communicated their enthusiasm. Was I delusional? A good workshop leader is a master of attentive listening, yet I must have been replaying episodes of *Criminal Minds* in my head to be so far off the mark in my recollection of what took place during that first evening of class.

In this workshop I provided typed, summary critiques of each submission, so I was able to retrieve my comments to Jim off the computer. My one-and-a-half pages of commentary gushed with honest praise, all the more meaningful because I confessed that, as a rule, I can't stand stories about cars, especially muscle cars like Mustangs. In my notes I had articulated my admiration for the psychological complexity of Jim's protagonist, his compelling plot, and the clarity of his language.

In one paragraph, I did suggest that Jim might want to edit with an eye toward trimming of the "as you know, Bob's," related to the history of Mustang performance. Authenticating background information is terrific, I reassured Jim, but long, technical explanations inserted into a character's thoughts or dialogue typically feel contrived to the reader and disrupt the flow of the narrative. I pointed out one example in Jim's story in which the protagonist reflects, for no apparent reason, on how the Mach 1 was introduced in 1969 with a 351, 390, or 428 V8 and a stiffer suspension; how manual drum brakes were standard at the time; and how the average new car had a top speed of 125 miles per hour and got 12 miles per gallon. A much better strategy, I suggested, would be to disperse some of this background information throughout the narrative, if and when it could be tethered to relevant moments in the plot.

"That said," I wrote in the conclusion of my critique, "a wonderful draft!"

After rereading my feedback, I asked myself again—*Was it me . . . or was it Jim?* I reread my notes. I reread them again.

It was Jim. Definitely Jim.

Writers, even as you are reading this chapter, I invite you to take a moment to formally acknowledge your predisposition to hypersensitivity. Own this characteristic shared by writers from prehistoric times to Jim—especially if you are *serious* about your work. "I am hypersensitive!" Say it loud. Say it proud.

The purpose of this admission is not to try to guilt feedback providers into going easy on you when critiquing your stories. In fact, professing your hypersensitivity as a writer may actually have the opposite effect, because it may be misinterpreted as an invitation to flick you upside the head. The purpose is to acknowledge that when it comes to that all-important question—Is it you . . . or is it them?—the answer is you. Definitely you. You. You. You. Yes, you.

And the sooner you own up to this fact, the sooner you will be able to see beyond the distraction of your own high dudgeon and focus on the feedback with more attention, acuity, and even appreciation.

Postscript

Jim's story had a happy ending. He completed the writing workshop, sold his Mustang story to a car-related publication, and continued to write fiction. In fact, about five years after we shared our first workshop, Jim phoned me out of the blue, asking to enroll again in the class. Now he was writing a historical novel set during the French and Indian War. "Just one thing," Jim cautioned as I enthusiastically welcomed him back. "Sometimes your group has a tendency to be too nice during the discussions, and I'm looking for *serious* feedback."

PROCESSING FEEDBACK

Here is what most writers forget: You are the boss of your own story. Not the other writers in your critique group. Not the famous author whose workshop you were lucky enough to get into at the Iowa Summer Writing Festival. Not even your mother-in-law who comes into your house while you are at work and vacuums the mattresses because somebody has to protect her grandchildren from dust mites. When it comes to applying feedback, you—and only you—are the one who gets to determine what stays and what goes in your story. And that is a good thing.

So why do most writers forget this fact? Why do most of us, when confronted with feedback, automatically relinquish authorial control and start scribbling copious notes all over our manuscripts like some junior intern on Red Bull, determined to meet everyone's demands. "Yes, sir, I'll rewrite the whole novel in first person and add more sex scenes, no problem." "No, ma'am, I don't need to kill off the grandfather in the end; I thought he was a nice guy, too." "Yes, sir, I'm sure my memoir would sell better if I were raised by wolves. I'll get on it right away."

When processing feedback, most of us need assertiveness training, if not for the sake of our stories then for our mental health. For one thing, you will never be able to please everybody anyway. Newton's third principle of motion explains that for every action there is an equal and opposite reaction, and any given writing workshop underscores this same reality. For instance, if your well-respected writing instructor hates the scene depicting your main character's long bus trip to Reno, it is inevitable that another respected feedback provider in that very same workshop—likely the graphic novelist / performance artist whom you have had a crush on since day one—will drill his tortured eyes into your soul and insist that the long bus trip is the one part of your story that rocked his world. So now what do you do?

There is only one thing you can do. When processing feedback you must plant yourself figuratively in the corner office, plunk down one of those "World's Best Boss" mugs on your desk, and claim creative control. Because if you don't, whenever you sit down to revise your work you are likely to start second-guessing and compromising and rewriting by committee until your story starts to read more like word salad than impassioned, polished prose.

Acknowledging that you are the boss of your own story makes processing feedback a lot more palatable, even when you are in the hot seat. Who doesn't have a silent meltdown when their pages are up for review, whether by a single reader or an entire writing workshop? I know when the time comes for my work to be critiqued, I always have a strong urge to toss back a few in the lav, if only to stop the soundtrack in my head. *They're gonna hate it, I know they're gonna hate it . . . Oh, I can already hear the workshop star, Roberta, with her usual refrain, "Kill your darlings . . ." (which she keeps stupidly attributing to Mark Twain). And Lars and those stupid bike shorts he wears to the meetings, always telling me to "use the active voice!" And Marilyn, throwing her twenty-thousand-dollar advance in my face and reminding me ad nauseam, "Add more conflict. Only trouble is interesting."*

But then I remind myself that I am the boss of my own story, so there is really no need to get all worked up in my head. If someone does trash my work—"Well, this is a sorry excuse for a story"—I can and should hold that person accountable. "What exactly do you mean by 'sorry excuse'? What part was sorry? Why was it sorry?" As the world's best boss, I should strive to be inclusive, encouraging all my readers to speak up and be forthright. I can listen to their comments with equanimity, even appreciation, knowing that soon I will return to my corner office, shut the door on the cacophony, and continue to process all feedback on my own time and in my own way.

Over the years I have calculated that feedback on any given piece of writing always falls into one of three categories and breaks down into the following percentages: 14 percent of feedback is dead-on; 18 percent is from another planet; and 68 percent falls somewhere in between. I am not a statistician (actually, I am hopeless in math), but I find it reassuring to know that there is an element of predictability to the art of processing feedback.

Dead-on feedback is the kind of feedback that feels right the moment you hear it, usually because it confirms something you already know on a gut level. *Oh, yeah,* you think when you hear dead-on feedback, *now I remember not liking that passage myself, but I was having such a good writing day I just kept going and forgot all about it.* Dead-on feedback is also the kind of feedback that can lead to those wonderful *Aha!* moments. For example, a reader might tell you that he isn't hooked by your story until the scene on page 8 when the surgeon amputates the wrong leg. For weeks you had been struggling with those opening pages that summarize the protagonist's medical-school education, trying and failing to get them right. Now, just like Archimedes in the bathtub, you see the solution all at once: *Cut the opening! Cut the opening! Start in medias res!* Processing dead-on feedback is easy because a small region of your brain—the right hemisphere anterior-superior temporal gyrus—flashes you the instant message: *Eureka!*

The 18 percent of feedback from another planet is also relatively easy to process once you catch on to the fact that the feedback provider has personal issues. See how long it takes you to figure out where this reader is coming from: "I think your main character should kill off her boyfriend. Why? Because men are pigs! All men are pigs! They're born pigs, they die pigs, and in between they give you a promise ring on Valentine's Day, but then they make out with your ex–best friend Sheena at Happy Hour two Fridays ago, and I know this for a fact because my new best friend Heather saw the whole thing while I was out in the parking lot throwing up after we did all those two-shots-for-two-dollars . . ." Feedback from another planet should be discounted for obvious reasons, but make sure you don't discount the provider along with it. She may still surprise you when critiquing your next story.

Which brings me to the remaining 68 percent of feedback, which falls somewhere in between dead-on feedback and feedback from another planet. This category of feedback may include a timid suggestion that speaks volumes about a weakness in your plot. It may include a brilliant insight that ends up being wrong for your current story but will certainly apply to another story down the road. Or it may include a blunt comment that raises your hackles along with the level of your prose.

One of the first things to look for when processing in-between feedback is a consensus of opinion. Say you present your work to three or four trusted readers and more than one of them found your ending confusing—Did the father reconcile with his teenage son, or didn't he? If your intention in the story is to clearly show a reconciliation, then you should pay particular attention to any type of collective opinion on this point. This doesn't mean you should automatically change your ending, but it does mean you should scrutinize your motives if you don't change it. Are you preserving the ending because you really think it works and is perfect as is or because you are being lazy or are overly attached to the writing?

Now take the same story, but a different scenario. Let's assume half your readers "got" the ending, but the other half didn't understand your intent. If this is the case, first you should feel good about batting .500. Then you should take the time to process the feedback from your excluded readers more carefully, just in case they offer any insights about how you might tweak or revise the ending to make it more accessible to a broader audience. For instance, Darla, the young woman in the group who brings her own "magic" candle to the meetings, offers the following feedback: "Honey, if you want us to know that father and his boy make up at the end of your story, why don't you just have them hug in the last scene?"

Your knee-jerk reaction to Darla's feedback may be to dismiss it outright because Darla writes paranormal romance and you are a snob. But part of processing feedback is getting over yourself and recognizing that sometimes feedback can be wrong in the particulars but right overall. Okay, so neither you nor the father in your story are huggers. But what if the father did show some outward sign of love for his son at the end? What if he offered the boy his prized penknife, for example, the one that his own father gave him when he left home as a teenager? That scene would maintain the integrity of the father's character, add a wonderful symbolic gesture, and clarify the ending for more readers.

Two of the biggest mistakes writers can make when processing feedback is to categorize readers too quickly (good reader / bad reader) and to do the same with their comments (good advice / bad advice). That's not how feedback works 68 percent of the time. As writers we have to be vigilant to fight the impulse to accept or ignore feedback wholesale. Just recently someone gave me some heavy-handed advice that I thought was totally ridiculous until I took the time to scale it down in service to my story.

Processing feedback effectively means being receptive to hearing a variety of opinions but filtering it all through your own writerly lens. What serves your intent? What rings true? What is your own inner voice telling you to do? Sometimes it can be hard to tune in to your own instincts after a feedback session, especially when the comments have been coming at you like the arrows flying at St. Sebastian. But that's when you need to hightail it to your corner office and drink from your World's Best Boss mug. Breathe. Give yourself some space and quiet. Listen carefully, and I promise you that your inner voice will speak up over time. And here is what it will tell you: 14 percent of the feedback feels dead-on, 18 percent is from another planet, and 68 percent feels like Darla, arms outstretched, coming at you with a magic candle. Just remember: Darla can comfort you or she can burn you. As boss of your own story, it is up to you to decide.

Tips for Processing Feedback

Be open: You can't begin to process feedback if you won't let it in. I know how hard it is to curb the impulse to defend your work against every little criticism, but try. If it helps, write a note on your palm as a reminder—*Hush up!*—and refer to it whenever you hear yourself debating your readers or saying things like, "I'm rubber and you're glue . . ." In a workshop setting, some groups institute a "no talking" policy to prevent writers from disrupting their own story critiques, but I feel that's an extreme measure. Writers should feel free to ask questions or raise issues that inform the discussion.

Resist the urge to explain: A teacher I know who works with both writers and actors once noted that if you tell a performer something didn't work in his performance, he simply drops the line or fixes it, whereas writers have a natural impulse to explain why they wrote something a certain way or what they were trying to communicate in the piece. As writers, we need to resist the urge to explain. Explanations give feedback providers too much information, making it harder for them to separate what is coming across on the page from what you have told them.

Little by little: People talk about the paralysis of the blank page, but they ignore the same reaction that can happen when faced with a full draft in need of an overhaul. To manage the overwhelming feeling that sometimes accompanies revision, remember you only need focus on addressing one issue at a time. What feedback resonated the most with your own instincts? Consider one aspect of the draft you know you want to rework, say amplifying the scenic moment on page 12 and moving it to the opening. Just revise the thing or things you are clear about. You can't know what you don't know, so set those other issues aside. They'll be waiting for you when you're ready to address them. Or maybe they'll already be solved when you were busy making other revisions.

Don't seek or act on feedback until it serves you: If you are on a roll with your writing, don't let feedback stop you. Some writers avoid feedback until they have taken their work as far as they can on their own. This makes sense if hearing feedback too soon interferes with your own creative vision. Just realize that feedback can also serve you in the midst of a productive period. The value of hearing feedback and then putting it in your mental lockbox as you push forward is that this allows your unconscious mind to quietly process the outside information in a way that informs your writing in sync with your instincts—without slowing you down.

Try out the feedback: Sometimes the only way to judge feedback is to play it out on the page where your own writerly instincts can react to it. For example, if a trusted reader is adamant that your first-person, coming-of-age novel should be written in third person, try writing a chapter this way. See for yourself what you lose or gain. If several readers think that your main character isn't likable, write a scene inside or outside the story that helps you and your readers better understand your protagonist's motives, vulnerabilities, or wants. Whether you ultimately use the scene or not, this is a great exercise in character development. No writing is a waste of effort.

Give yourself time: If you are at a point in the revision process where you can't tell whether you are making things better or worse—stop! Move away from the computer with your hands in the air before you do any permanent damage. Take a break from writing, or at the least move to another scene, or even start something brand new. It is remarkable how a good night's sleep or a short period away from the manuscript can restore clarity and help you process feedback in a way that leads to enlightenment.

SAMINA ALI:
"I WOULD HAVE SOLD MY SOUL."

When Samina Ali had forty pages written of what turned out to be her first novel, *Madras on Rainy Days,* she sent them to four agents. Within a week every one of them had phoned her, eager to take her on as a client. Third on the line was one of the top agents in the country, a woman based in Los Angeles, who started the conversation by gushing about Samina's writing. This agent repeatedly addressed Samina as "darling." She informed Samina she'd be sending a contract immediately—"just a formality." She promised to make Samina "the next hot thing."

"When I got her call I just flipped," says Samina, who was twenty-six at the time and a graduate of the MFA program at the University of Oregon. Samina had been writing scenes of the novel off and on since she was twenty, revising just the first chapter alone for two years. After graduate school she stopped writing completely for a year—"I had so many demons in my head"— but she ultimately returned to *Madras.* Forty pages later, Samina's phone was ringing. "It was so exciting to think this woman could be *my* agent," the author recalls. "I thought, you can't do any better than this."

"You know, Samina, darling," said the agent from LA, "There's a new 'F' word. Do you know what it is?"

Samina, embarrassed by her naiveté, racked her brain. "No . . ."

"Fiction," said the agent. "Darling, nobody writes fiction anymore." Samina would have to change her novel, some of which was based on her experience as a Muslim woman in an arranged marriage, to a memoir.

"But a lot of the novel isn't true," Samina explained to the agent.

"Do you think Maxine Hong Kingston's memoir is true?" the agent countered. "Do you think Frank McCourt's *Angela's Ashes* is true? They're not true; they're just marketed as true. And I don't want your book to have anything to do with you and your arranged marriage. I want it to be about you and your father."

Samina's mind was racing. What could she write about her father? "The book's not about my father," she apologized.

"Just write anything you want about *a* father. We'll collaborate, just as I collaborate with all my authors. No writer writes a book alone. We'll call your memoir *Demon Lover*. We'll write *Demon Lover* together!" The agent wanted a manuscript from Samina in ten months. *Ten months*, thought Samina. *I can do it!*

"We're not just going to sell *Demon Lover*," the agent went on. "We're going to sell Samina. Just *Samina!* No last name. You're gorgeous, darling. We're going to put you on the cover of every magazine. I want you to think big! Big! Don't just think of yourself as a writer, think of yourself as a rock star." Samina was spellbound by the agent's exuberance. A rock star! *Demon Lover!* By *Samina!*

The contract arrived from California the next day. Samina signed it, but this was the weekend so she would have to wait until Monday to drop it in the mail. On Sunday Samina received another call in the morning. This one was from the fourth agent she had queried. His name was Eric Simonoff, and he was a vice president of Janklow & Nesbit Associates in Manhattan. Eric had spent the previous night reading Samina's forty pages, and he was phoning her from his home. They spoke for over two hours.

"We talked about *my* book," says Samina. "It was the most refreshing, comfortable conversation. It was the first time I realized that stories are universal. It was startling to me that this white, Jewish man from New York related to a Muslim, feminist novel. I felt understood." Goodbye, *Demon Lover*. Welcome back, *Madras on Rainy Days*.

In hindsight, Samina can't believe how close she came to choosing the other agent, the star-maker from Los Angeles who called her "darling" and wanted her to write a memoir about a father, any father. "When you're young and impressionable, the process is very seductive," Samina cautions. "I remember thinking, this woman must know what she's doing; look at how famous her authors are. I can become *Samina!* When Eric called two days later," Samina says, "it was like this window opened up in my mind, and I felt like I'd been set free."

After their conversation that Sunday morning, Eric sent a contract to Samina the next day, and that's the one she unhesitatingly put in the mail. A very good move, Samina emphasizes, and not just because Eric later sold the completed manuscript to Farrar, Straus & Giroux, garnering her the largest advance this prestigious publisher had ever offered to a first-time author. The book also went on to be awarded the 2005 Prix Premier Roman Etranger (Best First Novel in Translation of the Year) by France and was also a finalist for the PEN/Hemingway Award in Fiction. Her debut also paved the way for her ongoing career as a writer and speaker.

"I really, really would have trapped myself in a very unhealthy relationship," Samina says of her near seduction by the other agent. "Who would have taken me seriously? Would Farrar have even considered *Demon Lover*? Would I have been on the cover of *Poets and Writers*? My career would have been over by now," Samina says. "I would have sold my soul."

TWENTY-TWO YEARS

One time I went with a friend of a friend to lunch, my treat, so I could pick his brain about feedback. This man was a children's librarian and aspiring author who had just received a knock-your-socks-off publishing deal for his first novel. I'm talking about the kind of offer the rest of us scribblers fantasize about incessantly when we should be working on our own novels, or at least on our abs. I'm talking hardcover and paperback rights from a major publishing house, a two-book contract, and the one thing that every writer craves more than anything else in the world—an advance large enough to give us an excuse to quit our day jobs. This friend of a friend had already given his notice at story hour.

When I spoke with this man about the manuscript for *Toxic Feedback*, the first thing he did was criticize the title. This was immediately followed by his assertion that when he was working on his own book he had never solicited feedback from anybody.

"Never?" I asked.

"Never ever," he assured me, brandishing a knife over his blackened chicken Caesar salad. After all, he explained, how could an outsider possibly have more insight into his book than he did?

Never ever. The notion gave me pause. Maybe this friend of a friend had a point. If you are the one who is writing the book, why *should* you trouble yourself with other people's opinions? From this man's perspective, my own book's premise—that feedback is a terrific resource you should capitalize on throughout the writing process—now seemed entirely stupid, as stupid, for example, as adding Red Dye #3 to pistachio nuts. Who needs it? Why bother?

In the end, you'll only end up with something unnatural, toxic, and needlessly messy. Suddenly, I experienced a crisis of confidence.

My crisis lasted until dessert. As this friend of a friend was enjoying his tiramisu, he casually mentioned that it had taken him twenty-two years to complete his novel. Yes, I had heard him correctly. Twenty-two years. That's two decades, going on three. Time enough to see five presidents come and go in the Oval Office, the evolution of YouTube from a single, eighteen-second video of an elephant to over two million cat videos, and a film version of *Charlie's Angels*—plus a sequel. Such a span of time doesn't necessarily imply any dysfunction in the writer or his work habits (after all, writing is not a race), except for this one additional fact shared by this friend of a friend. During those two decades he labored on his novel, he also experienced extended, want-to-put-your-head-through-the-plaster bouts of writer's block, self-doubt, and boredom.

Nothing could have cheered me up more. In fact, now I recognized this man as a veritable poster child for *Toxic Feedback;* the embodiment of my book's target audience. I understand that novelists, or writers of any kind, need to allow time for their ideas and stories to gestate without interference from busybody, opinionated feedback providers. I am also not arguing the fact that this man is an excellent writer who should defer to his own editorial judgment during the revision process. But twenty-two years. Think about how much angst he might have avoided, how many other novels he might have produced, how much happier the childhood of his now-grown sons might have been over the course of those two decades if he hadn't been so fanatical about squirreling away his work-in-progress. Despite the cliché, time is not on our side. As this writer said to his own agent, whom he temporarily fired when the woman failed to send his manuscript to publishers at a pace to his liking, "I'm not getting any younger."

Certainly there will always be dry spells during the writing process. In truth, I think short, agonizing episodes of writer's block, self-doubt, and boredom are actually healthy by-products of the creative process; your unconscious's way of saying, *Hey, Mr. Thinks-He-Knows-Everything, stop pestering me for a while so I can sort out this plot in peace.* But I would suggest that *extended* bouts of writer's block, self-doubt, and boredom are not a healthy part of the creative process. I am talking about those bleak periods that go on for weeks, maybe months, maybe years, when writers find themselves asking, *Why? Why am I doing this? Shouldn't I be spending my six minutes of free time doing something that is actually important, like teaching my eleven-year-old to read?* These are the dark days when soliciting feedback is most important.

People typically turn to feedback for help with editing. For example, what could be better than an outside perspective to quickly alert you to the fact that your opening chapter, as precious as it is, is spoiled rotten and could use some solid discipline—say editing down the first seventy-four pages of description about the narrator's breach birth to a single declarative sentence? But the value of feedback isn't limited to advice about structure and wordsmithing. Feedback is just as much about bolstering the writer's faith in himself and excitement about his project along the way. It is about getting some external validation.

Let's say your manuscript is a hot mess and you don't have a clue where to go from here. At this point, the best thing you can do is to show your work to someone, maybe a trusted friend, or an online critique group, or perhaps even a lively, healthy workshop in your community. Once you do this, your readers will inevitably begin talking about the characters you made up as if they are real. (Okay, most of them are thinly disguised depictions of your relatives, but that's irrelevant at the moment.) Your readers will let you know, in no uncertain terms, that they collectively despise (in a most satisfying way) your story's antagonist, Frieda, the heiress who is determined to destroy your heroine's life. They will express grief over the secret past of your narrator, Martin, that prevents him from committing to his lover. The men in the group will passionately defend the authenticity of your character Cindi, the pilot, who manages to safely land the plane in a blizzard, while the women in the group will insist she could have done so without the author mentioning the way her uniform clung to her curves. Debates will ensue, literary and otherwise. "What happens next?" the group will demand. "When can we see more?" they will ask.

With this kind of fresh perspective, a writer sees what is so hard to recognize when working in a vacuum. Your stories, even in the messy draft stage, can entertain people. Engage them in heated debates. Move them. Make them curious. Enable them to connect with someone or with an experience outside their normal realm. Writing—including writing-in-progress—nourishes and enlivens the human spirit, yours and your readers'.

Armed with these affirmations, you can return to your work with renewed confidence and vigor. You may make a lot of progress, or maybe just a little, but either way you will be better off than you were before, suffering in silence while the seasons changed. And every time you feel lost or bored for an unnatural period of time, you can renew your faith with more feedback—and more reminders from readers that your writing matters. Because it really does, and no one should wait twenty-two years to hear that.

Postscript: Tuesdays with Marjorie

Why the heck didn't I do this ages ago? I'm talking about my relatively recent arrangement with my writer-friend Marjorie, where we meet every Tuesday (more or less) to either write together, brainstorm ideas, talk about which bars have the best pours, commiserate about writing-related issues, offer feedback, or simply give each other weekly deadlines with a friendly face on the other side.

In the absence of a critique group or workshop, this kind of consistent support has made a huge difference in my writing life, in terms of both productivity and perspective. I never don't leave a meeting with Marjorie without feeling better. And that previous sentence reminds me of another value of this kind of partnership, which is that you have someone who will tell you the things you don't want to hear (like how you might have an addiction to double negatives), but you never don't mind hearing it from them.

Is there a trusted writer-friend you can invite into a similar partnership with weekly meet-ups, or even just phone check-ins? I hope so, because it's made my Tuesdays so much nicer.

EDITING YOUR EDITOR

In the original version of the game show *Who Wants to Be a Millionaire,* the young man in the hot seat was stumped by the following question, worth sixty-four thousand dollars: "What color does litmus paper turn when it comes into contact with acid—red, blue, green, or yellow?" The contestant stroked his chin and thought for a few, prolonged moments. Then he told Regis and millions of viewers he was pretty sure the answer was red. He had even worked one summer in a lab. But since sixty-four thousand dollars was at stake, he thought he had better use one of his lifelines to phone a friend. (The show gives contestants three "lifelines" to outside help, one of which is phone-a-friend.) So the contestant read the question aloud to his lifeline, who responded immediately, "Blue. Litmus paper comes in red and blue, so when it comes in contact with acid it turns blue or stays blue."

"Are you sure?" the contestant asked. All his instincts were still telling him the answer was red.

"I'm sure about this, buddy; the answer is blue."

"Blue," the contestant told Regis and millions of viewers.

"Final answer?" asked Regis.

"Final answer!" the contestant declared, gripping his armrests.

Of course, the answer was red. So it's only money, right? But that's not the point of this story. The point is that the lifeline spoke with authority. The lifeline only wanted what was best for his buddy. The lifeline was an intelligent guy (after all, you don't get selected as a phone-a-friend for your looks). All this goes to show that if your authoritative, well-meaning, intelligent lifeline can be wrong, then so can just about anybody.

Even your editor.

Editors are like lifelines to writers. They exist to save us from the embarrassment of obfuscation, sentimentality, saggy middles, misplaced modifiers, and other detractions that can cling to a manuscript like toilet paper to a shoe. What's more, editors read everything and know the market. This makes them book *experts* as well as a perfect test audience for how your book is going to hold up when it is on a store shelf surrounded by thousands of eye-catching tomes, most of them written by James Patterson, James Patterson with a coauthor, or a diet guru who once helped Oprah run a marathon. So if your editor at the publishing house actually makes the effort to write you a single-spaced, twelve-page, editorial letter chock-full of suggestions, consider yourself very, very lucky. But remember, if she says "blue" and all your instincts say "red," don't feel like you have to go along with her suggestions.

I used to be intimidated by editors. Actually, I still am intimidated by editors, and with good reason, I might add. Editors have a lot of authority. After all, it was your editor who acquired your book in the first place, or at least ratcheted it up the wheel of decision makers. So who is to say that if you displease her in any way, perhaps by looking askance at her suggestion to make your ending more upbeat, that she won't have your publishing contract yanked faster than you blew through that first part of the advance on dinner and beer at Buffalo Wild Wings?

Editors even intimate this possibility in legalese: *Should the publisher, in its sole judgment, conclude that the Work as first submitted cannot be revised to its satisfaction within a timely period, or after the agreed revision period, should the publisher find that the revised Work is still unacceptable for any editorial reason relating to the Work, the publisher may reject the Work by written notice to Proprietor.* My goodness, no wonder I never read my publishing contracts. And no wonder one of the most common questions aspiring authors ask published authors is, "Did your editor make you change stuff in your book?"

On the one hand, I think it is silly to worry in advance about whether some future editor is going to pull rank on your artistic integrity. That kind of fear will only hobble your courage to even try for publication. And let's get real: if you are that far along in the publishing process, you are probably a lot better off than you were a year or twelve ago when no editor cared about your depressing (read "unmarketable") ending, or the conversational style of your prose, or the unpronounceable name of your main character.

On the other hand, as the person who sweat blood over the manuscript and whose name will be on the cover, you are right to be paranoid, just in case there may be something to be paranoid about. I was eager for clarity on how much authority editors at publishing houses really have over our manuscripts, so I called up Carrie Thornton, editorial director of Three Rivers Press (part of the Crown Publishing Group / Random House). Here is our conversation:

Me: Can an editor make you change stuff in your book?

Carrie: No.

Me: Really! Why not?

Carrie: I can't just say to authors, "Do this" or "Do that," because, at the end of the day, it's their work, so that would be doing a shady thing.

Me: But what if it is something you *really* don't like?

Carrie: The most I've said is, "Fine, if you want to get bad reviews, we'll do it your way." But it takes a lot to get to that point. Most writers are open to suggestions, and I don't suggest anything without explaining why.

Me: And if they still disagree?

Carrie: I'm happy to listen. I'm happy to be wrong when the writer convinces me his way is better. I understand what's at stake emotionally for the writer.

Me: So you won't yank a contract over an editorial disagreement? [Note: As you can probably tell, my style of journalism is to repeat the same question over and over, slightly reworded, until I am convinced of the answer.]

Carrie: Editors can cancel a contract for nondelivery, or if a book is just not what was described in the contract. For example, if I commissioned a book on dog training and the writer turned in a book on how to buy a dog. But for an editorial dispute, I can't imagine canceling a contract. Once you've made the financial commitment to the writer, you want to do everything you can to publish the book because, honestly, we'd be the ones to lose money.

I found my conversation with Carrie tremendously reassuring. In retrospect, I realized that my own experiences working with editors had mirrored what Carrie had said. I have had editorial disagreements with editors at three different publishing houses (independent, giant, and academic), yet none of them ever acted the bully, and each one offered helpful suggestions.

In addition, I have come to understand that even at the copy-editing stage, few, if any, copy editors make what are called "silent changes," that is, changes to your words, or even misspellings, without alerting you to their suggestions or corrections.

Most of the writers I talked to for this book also enjoyed good relationships with their editors. Yes, there were a few unhappy stories. One writer told me how the editor who had "inherited" her book (after the acquiring editor took another job) treated it like an unwanted orphan. Some writers were surprised at how little their editors actually edited. And, of course, every profession has its share of psychopaths.

Still, I think it is safe to assume that aspiring authors (and this includes authors like myself who aspire to continue publishing) can let go of their paranoia about editor-despots and focus on a more relevant question: How can writers make the most of their working relationship with editors? What follows are some suggestions that can be applied to working with *any* editor, whether it is the one who acquired your book for publication or someone you hired to help whip your manuscript into shape before you seek publication.

Think collaboration: Don't forget, you and your editor are on the same side, sharing the mutual goal of producing the best book possible. You bring to the collaboration the vision, the voice, and a familiarity with the work that only comes from spending umpteen hours laboring over its creation. Your editor contributes a reader's perspective, professional editing skills, and a knowledge of how to size and price your book for the market. When your editor makes suggestions, be open. Be respectful. Aim to please, but don't pander.

Expect guidance, not fixes: Editors edit at two levels. They look at the big-picture issues such as pacing and development. And they look at the language—Is the wording clear? Where is there repetition or flab? In either case, most editors (with the exception of copy editors) are more likely to make general comments, pointing out patterns and a few supporting examples, rather than say, "Do this," or, "Fix that." As one editor told me, "I expect and hope that writers will take a fair amount of responsibility in the revision process."

Wait: An editor once suggested a major structural change in my manuscript that I hated. Immediately, I composed an email rebuttal, the gist of it being that she was WRONG! WRONG! WRONG! Thankfully, I didn't push "Send," partly because the stakes were so high I was afraid of her response. This gave me time to revise my note over the next few days, fleshing out my argument and toning down the vitriol. When I eventually did send the email, my heart was racing. Only a few hours later the editor responded, "I see your point. I'm fine with the structure as is."

Picture your editor's life: Eleven new proposals just landed on her desk, adding to the fourteen she didn't have time to respond to yesterday. She's got your book to edit along with several others, all with various production timetables that can't be compromised. At lunch she needs to dash to Macy's to try on bathing suits under fluorescent lighting, then race to a three-hour meeting with sales and marketing. Oh, and last night she was up until 2:00 a.m. with a sick kid and a stack of trade journals that she never found time to read. Bear all this in mind when you consider her editorial judgment and the pace at which she returns your phone calls.

Give and take: When it comes to making editorial changes, it never hurts to give a little. In fact, it helps. Once you show your editor you aren't poised to fight every suggestion, she's likely to be more cooperative than commanding, especially when she hears the finality in your voice about the issues that really matter to you. "Throw 'em a bone, for Chrissakes," is how one author put it (but he writes crime novels, so that might be his police lieutenant talking).

Be a problem solver, not problem creator: "The most frustrating thing a writer can do is to consistently disagree with my suggestions, but not offer any alternatives," said one editor. "'I hate the subtitle. I hate the subtitle.' So then come up with an alternative," he advises. "The process is supposed to be an exchange of ideas."

Don't go to great lengths: I was surprised when an editor informed me that publishers feel as strongly about the length of a book as they do about its editorial treatment. That was until I learned that if a manuscript comes in just 10 percent over word count, the editor has to justify it to the folks in accounting. Books are made up of "signatures" of (usually) eight pages each; adding just another page amounts to adding an additional seven pages, which in turn translates to higher production costs. Given this reality, be sure to take your contractual word count seriously and be open to trimming if your book comes in long. Publishers aren't likely to absorb the additional expenses of an oversized, over-budget tome unless, of course, it's written by Barack Obama or the ghost of Tolstoy.

Show good manners: An author friend was working with her editor on revisions to her book. They had to work fast to meet her publishing deadline. My friend got behind on her rewrites by about a week, so she phoned the editor to tell her not to expect the new pages on time. The editor was stunned. "You're the first author who has ever proactively let me know she's behind," the editor told her. "Usually they just stop taking my calls."

Bundle: As much as you would like to instant message your editor every five seconds to make sure your revisions are on target and she still thinks the world of you, busy editors would prefer it if you bundled your reactions and questions into one longer email or phone conversation. Otherwise, they really might stop loving you.

Be forceful and articulate: In my first book, my editor's boss wanted me to take out all the profanity, or at least replace the middle letters with asterisks. This would have been a great idea had I been shooting for the children's market, but this was a book of diary entries from real women. So even though I was a nervous wreck about coming off as one of those pushy first-time authors, not to mention a gutter mouth, I reiterated my argument over the course of several weeks until my editor's boss reluctantly conceded. A few years later I was talking with my former editor (we no longer work together but have remained friends) when she brought up this debate over swear words. "Thank you for being so forceful and articulate," she said. "Your arguments really helped me convince my boss." *Forceful and articulate.* This took me by surprise and taught me a good lesson about working with editors, because the whole time I was fighting to preserve my book's integrity, I thought my editor thought I was just being a pain in the a**!

ERNEST HEBERT:
"I WANTED WRITING TO BE EASY
FOR ME AND IT WASN'T."

In 1974 Ernest Hebert's wife, Medora, dragged him to the Bread Loaf Writers' Conference. They couldn't afford it—in fact, money was so tight they had to camp out for the two weeks of the conference—but Ernie knew he needed some instruction. "Something was wrong with my method of composition, but I didn't know what," Ernie says, "and I certainly wasn't making any progress in the material world." Ernie was thirty-three years old when he reluctantly agreed to go to Bread Loaf, and he had only published a single short story in college. Since then, he'd started a couple of projects, finished a lousy novel, and was drifting. "I would have quit," Ernie says, "but every once in a while I'd write one good paragraph and then I'd think, *If I can write one, I can write fifty*."

Ernie's assigned faculty reader at Bread Loaf was the noted writer and critic John Gardner, author of *The Art of Fiction* and *On Becoming a Novelist*. A few months before the conference, Ernie had submitted a manuscript for critique, a clean-typed first draft, sixty pages long, single spaced, "straight out of my id," he says. Gardner was scheduled to meet with Ernie to critique the work for a half hour on the last day of the conference. In the weeks before the meeting, Ernie was in a state of total anxiety, held together by his wife and another writer, Bill Atwill, whom he had met at the conference. "Some of the other writers there saw Bread Loaf as a vacation," Ernie says. "I hated them all because I was in a crisis and all these people were treating it like fun."

Ernie showed up at the appointed time for his meeting with his faculty reader. "I remember Gardner's face," Ernie says. "He was very blond and fair. From the profile, he looked almost pretty, feminine. Square on, he looked hard, Gestapo-like." The two men shook hands. Then Gardner picked up Ernie's thick, single-spaced manuscript, pointed to a spot about a third of the way down the first page, and said, "This is as far as I read. No real writer would write a sentence like that." End of meeting.

"It wasn't that I wanted to defend myself," Ernie says. "I was incapable of breathing. I could barely get up to leave. Gardner was happy to see me leave." Ernie never looked at that manuscript again.

When he returned home from the conference, Ernie thought about some of the themes from Gardner's lectures at Bread Loaf. *You can't just write a crummy first draft. Write every scene as if it's the only scene in the book. One bad scene is nothing but a take-off for the next bad scene.* "I began to see the wisdom of that," Ernie says. "I remembered that the things I'd written well had been written over and over. I wanted writing to be easy for me and it wasn't."

The meeting with Gardner changed Ernie's perspective. "I was hurt, but not tense anymore. I was born again." He decided he wasn't going to worry about writing a novel. For a while, an idea for a character had been demanding his attention—a small-town man outside the middle class. Ernie decided to find out more about this fellow. "I wrote longhand, typed, pencil-edited, re-typed. I told myself I wouldn't move on until each section was brilliant, with at least one striking metaphor or turn on every page."

The character Ernie created was Howard Elman, the protagonist of his first novel, *The Dogs of March,* the cornerstone of the author's acclaimed seven-book Darby series set in rural New England. The *Washington Post Book World* described the novel as "a human story in which each page offers some new insight into the human mind and heart." Today, *The Dogs of March* is still in print and continues to be taught at colleges and high schools across the country. Ernie is also the author of *The Old American,* hailed by *Kirkus Reviews* as "a brilliant work." Most recently, at age eighty, he published his eleventh book, *Whirlybird Island,* technically not part of his renowned Darby Chronicles but set in a similar landscape.

"Gardner was probably right," Ernie says, referring to that sixty-page, single-spaced first draft he shared with the legendary critic decades ago. "The piece was hastily put together, not very good writing. Since then my rule has been never to show anything to anybody until I have done my best work. On occasion I've broken this rule, always to my regret."

FEEDBACK HOTLINES

One of the hardest things for me is finding the time to write. Family responsibilities, jobs that pay the bills, cute animal videos, life . . . all of these things conspire to whittle away at my writing time until I am lucky if I salvage a few hours per day for getting some words on paper. And things were even more challenging when my daughters were little. I recall thinking that if by some miracle I was able to sneak in some extra time at the computer, maybe after my youngest daughter got home from kindergarten, I'd better make it count because the clock was ticking, I needed to be an efficiency machine, and *The Little Mermaid* only ran for eighty-three minutes! (Why couldn't Disney make these movies any longer?)

Sadly, I am not an efficiency machine, at least not when it comes to writing. This is partly because the creative process doesn't lend itself to efficiency, at least not in the same way that I can efficiently catch up on all the *People* magazines at the hair salon or finish off a carton of mint chocolate chip ice cream without even dirtying a bowl. Even when I come to the computer with a clear vision of what I want to say, my brain often seizes up as soon as I try to translate my thoughts into standard English. Or I'll start out okay, but then I find myself imprisoned in some tricky paragraph, writing it over and over again. Or I'll reread a finished chapter, but by this time it all sounds so predictable that I become convinced I must have plagiarized some tiresome author I was assigned back in junior high school. Meanwhile, ticktock, ticktock, ticktock. I am stuck inside my own head, panic is setting in, and I have flashbacks of that little mermaid Ariel, racing through her movie like she's some kind of cokehead.

That's when I pick up the phone and call a feedback hotline.

If you have ever experienced a difficult writing session (and if you haven't, I don't want to hear about it), you know how a slow start or stall-out can feel like a mini-crisis. And let's face it, most writers, by temperament, are not very good in a crisis, because our first instinct at any sign of trouble is to do something desperate like take a nap or clean our toilets. Oddly enough, these mindless distractions can occasionally serve the creative process. But, to paraphrase Freud, sometimes a distraction is just a distraction, which is why a feedback hotline offers a great alternative. With one relatively quick, well-placed call, you just may get the information, or reality check, or spark of inspiration you need to push your way through to a productive work session.

As the name implies, a feedback hotline gives you direct access to help with whatever psychological or linguistical crisis you are facing *at the moment*. No, there is no national, toll-free hotline that provides this service to distraught writers (though now that I think of it, there should be). You can, however, easily establish your own hotline by engaging any friends who care about your mental health and want to see you succeed, or by availing yourself of other resources such as teachers, workshop peers, or experts in the field who don't mind the occasional crisis call or who are too cheap to spring for caller ID.

Here, I want to emphasize that even if the first number in your feedback hotline's speed-dial connects you to your best friend's cell phone, you should never use the hotline for social calls or a gabfest. This is a writing resource, one in which you scream *"Help!"* and the voice on the other end of the line obliges with the appropriate form of feedback. Maybe you are having trouble organizing your thoughts and could use some guidance as to how to start. Maybe you are stuck on a Gordian plot point and want to brainstorm "What-ifs." Maybe you have lost your sense of humor and need a reminder why you should *not* have that CBD-infused martini with the citrus twist at 10:00 a.m. (No, the garnish does not qualify as part of any healthy food group.) Regardless, both you and your feedback hotline need to stay focused on the writing issue at hand; and the very second you feel like you have achieved any kind of breakthrough, you need to hang up the phone and push on with your writing. Don't worry about saying goodbye or other pleasantries. Your hotline will understand. Clarity is fleeting, so you don't want to waste precious seconds.

One of my own favorite feedback hotlines is my friend Nancy, whom I met years ago in graduate school when I sat one row above her in a tiered-seating classroom. It was the summer term, and I had fallen off my bike the day before, which meant my raw, bloodied knees aligned exactly with her line of vision whenever she swiveled her chair. This made for a natural conversation starter that led to a long-lasting friendship. Nancy actually inspired the feedback hotline concept several years ago when she was working as a researcher at a technology corporation and I was struggling with an essay that was due all too soon at *The Writer* magazine, of all places.

For some reason this particular assignment overwhelmed me, maybe because I felt so passionate about the topic. One morning, in the midst of yet another frustrating, nonwriting session, I picked up the phone and called Nancy at work, partly to stave off panic and partly to see if she could meet me for an early lunch. But instead of debating the merits of Thai versus sushi, I started ranting about my writing assignment. Nancy offered me a sounding board for my scattered thoughts. She didn't make me feel like an idiot for needing help. She asked questions and offered insights that helped me organize my thoughts. In essence, she turned my spontaneous rant into a productive work session. Toward the end of our conversation, when I was telling Nancy about my idea for a lede for the essay, she responded, "Why don't you just write it down exactly like you told me?" So I hung up the phone and did just that.

That's when the value of having a feedback hotline first occurred to me. As insurance that I would continue to make progress on my assignment and meet my deadline, I asked Nancy if I could call her whenever I felt like I needed an outside perspective. This arrangement worked well for both of us because I couldn't afford to waste any time, and she hated her boring job. Unless I called during the minigolf tournaments her office held every Friday in the hallways, she welcomed my creative diversions. Sometimes I'd phone Nancy several mornings in a row to jump-start my thinking. Sometimes I wouldn't call for weeks because I was on a roll. Sometimes I'd just email a quick question. Regardless, it always amazed me how even the smallest doses of feedback during a stagnant writing session could restore my emotional equilibrium and motivate my writing.

Unfortunately, a few months after Nancy started serving as my feedback hotline, she quit her boring job and found new, more fulfilling employment. This cut down on her availability during my working hours and forced me to broaden my network of feedback hotlines as I moved on to new writing projects. The big upside of this change, however, is that now I can pick and choose among my hotline resources depending on what type of feedback I require at that moment.

So now when my mind has gone blank, I often contact Meredith, because Meredith is a scientist-pagan-novelist who knows something interesting about everything.

Or I'll call Lois, who writes powerful poetry and is in her late eighties, because when Lois doesn't like something I've written she tells me bluntly, and how can I get mad at someone in her eighties?

Or I'll text Deb, a no-nonsense editor who actually came over to my house in response to one of my cries for help and decluttered my desk drowning in pages.

Or I'll call John, an academic, because he is the smartest book person I know in real life, which makes him the perfect test subject for my half-baked ideas.

Or I'll email Beth, an army sergeant once stationed at Saddam Hussein's presidential palace, because Beth writes honest, funny prose and stops me from being too writerly or sounding like Madonna with that faux British accent.

Or I'll message Helmut, my partner, to ask him to pick up a pizza because I am *this* close to achieving a breakthrough on my own.

Or I'll reach out to Mary, who wrote a critically acclaimed memoir and consults with companies about workplace discrimination, because Mary converses in eloquent, full sentences and always, always knows just the right words. For example, when I was talking with her about this chapter, fumbling to explain what I meant by a feedback hotline, Mary easily responded, "Oh yes, I also relied on several interlocutors while writing my memoir." This perfectly exemplifies the value of feedback hotlines and speaks to why you, too, should use them when you are immobilized at your desk and feel like you are going batty or wasting time. Because without *interlocutors* to help in a crisis, it would have taken me forever to think up that word.

"DANGER, DANGER,
WILL ROBINSON!"

So here I am in the bustling lobby of Big Time Publishers in New York City. I am here with my two partners in the book project *This Day in the Life* to meet with an editor from Big Time who told our agent she loves our proposal and wants to discuss it with us in person. As I am going through the building's security checkpoints, then standing in line to receive my identification badge, then elevating up sixty-seven floors at warp speed, then proceeding down a maze of halls to a tiny holding area with a wall of backlit books and a male receptionist in a dazzling white shirt, I have to keep telling myself this is really real. An editor at Big Time Publishers loves our proposal!

In what seemed like a lifetime ago, I'd had an idea for a book. I had wanted to know what a day in the life was really like for women from all walks of life—young, old, across races and ethnicities, rich, poor, stable, and high strung like me. How in the world, for example, can someone possibly be a funeral director? When I used to have an office job, I couldn't even stand being around coworkers, but at least they weren't corpses. And what about single moms? With those kinds of demands on my time, I think I'd be getting high on glue sticks every chance I got. Or what about Miss America? The perks! But can you imagine sporting a crown whenever you went out in public? I feel self-conscious just wearing big earrings.

When I had first envisioned this book, I knew I didn't want to interview women and write about their lives. What I wanted was to spend a day in their presence and in their heads. To that end, I decided I would ask hundreds of women across America to create a "day diary" on the very same day, jotting down not only what they were doing but also what they were thinking and feeling as they went through the course of that day. The book would be an edited collection of these first-person, real-time accounts.

Of course, it is one thing to have an idea. It is quite another thing to turn that idea into a reality, especially given the logistics involved in putting together a book of this nature. To make sure I didn't give up before I even started trying, I invited two friends, Becky Joffrey and Bindi Rakhra, to be my partners in the project.

Now here the three of us are, in New York City, following the beacon of the male receptionist's dazzling white shirt into the Big Time editor's office. I take a seat on her cozy couch under a voracious potted palm with an overhanging frond that keeps grazing my forehead. The editor who loves our proposal arrives and sinks into the cushion next to me. She is the epitome of today's hot, young literati—five minutes out of a prestigious women's college, exuding self-assurance, and fashionably concave in her ribbed black turtleneck, skinny skirt, and pointy-toed boots. Next to this woman I feel like her peasant grandmother who just arrived from the North Country. A copy of our book proposal rests on her lap. I peer under the frond and try to read the notes she has jotted in the margins.

"You have a fabulous concept for a book," the editor tells us. After having weathered an avalanche of rejections from other publishers, it takes all my reserve (of which I have painfully little, even in the best of circumstances) not to burst into joyful tears and kiss this woman's pointy-toed black boots. In fact, I am a bit stunned by her manner, which is warm and hardly fakey at all. I don't know what I was expecting, but it wasn't this . . . this *humanity*. Not from someone who works at Big Time Publishers, perpetuated in the press as some bottom-line-driven megacorpglomeration sprung from so many mergers and acquisitions that no one is really quite sure who owns it anymore.

The editor makes a few more enthusiastic comments about our proposal, and I beam beatifically. Maybe I am getting a little ahead of myself, but I start anticipating how I am going to let everyone in the world who ever thought I was a loser know that I am a Big Time author. That's right, *me*, a Big Time author, baby. *Big Time!*

The editor starts explaining how she envisions turning our proposal into a book. "Celebrities!" she announces brightly, and I sit up straighter, the frond poking me in the eye. At first I think she means me and my partners are going to be celebrities, but then I realize she is talking about the focus of our book. Only it is not our book, but a strange distortion of our book that she is describing. She elaborates, "Readers love celebrities. Readers don't care about ordinary people. Ordinary people don't sell books. Celebrities sell books. How about . . . *A Day in the Life of Celebrities!*"

When I was a kid, I used to watch reruns of an old sci-fi television show called *Lost in Space*. Now, sitting here in this Big Time editor's office, a line from that show pops into my head, "Danger, danger, Will Robinson!" In my mind's eye I can perfectly see the hokey little robot that used to spin and flail its metal arms in young Will Robinson's direction, trying to protect the poor kid from harm. Why is this editor talking about celebrities? I don't care about celebrities. I mean, I do seem to spend a lot of time clicking on links to celebrity breaking news, but my book idea has nothing to do with celebrities. What happened to the book described in our proposal, the very same proposal this editor professed to love and that is now resting on her lap? What happened to the book I envisioned?

Having had several years now to calm down after this meeting, I can tell you exactly what happened to that book I envisioned. It *almost* got lost in space. This Big Time editor, the one with the compliments and the cozy couch, really did love my book concept. Or rather, she loved the overall idea of using first-person, real-time accounts to reveal a day in the life. So this editor took my idea and creatively ran with it, supplanting my vision with hers. This editor was a vision supplanter, and out there—from big-city publishing houses to small-town critique groups—lurk thousands of others just like her.

Writers beware. Whenever you show a work-in-progress you are bound to encounter vision supplanters. These are feedback providers who can't help but view other people's ideas through their own creative lens. I see this happen all the time in my own writing workshops, with me being the biggest offender. Show me a draft with promise and I start burbling, "Play out the plot this way . . . Make the character that way . . . Now here's how you should end the story!" When I am on a tear like this, saying vision-supplanting things, this is what the writer should be hearing: "Danger, danger, Will Robinson!"

Vision supplanters, myself included, don't mean you or your writing any harm. We are motivated by our excitement about the potential of your work. We are sincere in wanting to help you make your story or poem better, more powerful, more like the way we would write it if we were lucky enough to have thought of it in the first place. This makes us all the more dangerous. I spoke with an editor at a small publishing house who often works with first-time authors of inspirational books. She told me that so many writers turned in manuscripts that failed to reflect the vision of their original proposal that she started telling the new writers she signed not to show their work to anyone during the writing process.

Obviously I don't agree with this advice (and later in the conversation the editor herself endorsed the value of feedback), but it does speak to how susceptible writers can be to other people's opinions, and how easy it is for feedback providers to forget whose work it is. One example comes from a friend of mine in a poetry group, where each week one member of the group would rewrite her colleague's previously submitted poems in an effort to show them what was best. Another example comes from a business professor I know who is equally passionate about history and hostile takeovers. He envisioned a book that used the rise and fall of historical empires to illuminate strategies for contemporary global business empires. "Great idea!" enthused one of his colleagues after reading the professor's first draft, "Now lose the history and the book will really sell."

During the writing process, you can and should rely on outsiders to help you rethink and revise many aspects of your writing. But your vision for the work is the one aspect that should remain yours and yours alone. Just like you can't borrow someone else's prescription glasses to see things more clearly, you also cannot use someone else's vision for your own work and expect to write with originality or strength of purpose. Your vision is what motivated you to write about the idea in the first place. Your vision is what allows you to take one of the thirty-six dramatic situations (purported by French critic Georges Polti to represent the entire spectrum of literary plots) and make it uniquely your own. Your vision is what infuses your poetry with passion and integrity.

Your vision is also what feeds your determination during the creative process. Even on the most discouraging writing days, when it feels like no one else believes in your idea, or like someone has rearranged all the letters on your keyboard to produce nothing but gibberish, your vision is the one thing that can compel you to keep trying. You know you have a compelling idea. You know there is something you really feel needs to be expressed, something you have to say. With your vision you can *see* it, even if you can't yet find the right words.

My vision for the *This Day in the Life* series was inspired by personal experiences. When I thought up the concept for that first book, I was feeling blue and needed to connect with other women. I also saw the project as a way for readers to get to know women beyond the reductive labels society assigns them, or that we assign ourselves. I wanted this collection of day diaries to show how unique and interesting we *all* are—in particular, those of us who are not celebrities.

When my partners and I left our meeting at Big Time Publishers, I really didn't know what to do. As a writer desperate for a publisher, I couldn't imagine turning down an offer from one of the biggest publishing houses in the world. But as a writer with a vision, I couldn't imagine accepting an offer that compromised everything that mattered to me about my idea.

Danger, danger, Will Robinson . . .

In the end, I didn't have to make the choice. Two weeks after our meeting, Big Time Publishers turned down our book proposal. In an email to our agent, the editor remained enthusiastic and gracious. "I love the idea behind *This Day in the Life* and think a book with this concept—especially one about celebrities—would be fantastic. Unfortunately, we just can't get our numbers to work so reluctantly we're going to be passing."

As a writer it is never easy to get rejected, especially from Big Time Publishers. In this particular instance, however, I believe that out there, somewhere in the publishing cosmos, a little robot must have been spinning around and flailing its metal arms in my direction, making sure I didn't lose my way.

JENNIFER CRUSIE:
"A STORY IS A COLLABORATION
BETWEEN A WRITER AND A
READER."

In the summer of 1991 Jennifer Crusie set a goal of reading a hundred romance novels as research for her dissertation on the impact of gender in narrative strategies. The experience taught her two things: reading romance novels made her feel good; and she wanted to try writing one herself. A year later she had quit her job as a high school English teacher to write full time, put her dissertation on hold, and sold her first book, *Sizzle,* to Silhouette. Next came over half a dozen books sold to Harlequin, including *Getting Rid of Bradley,* which earned her a Rita Award for Best Short Contemporary from the Romance Writers of America.

In 1995 Jennifer began to write mainstream novels for St. Martin's Press (*Tell Me Lies, Crazy for You, Faking It,* and *Bet Me,* to name a few of her best sellers), but don't assume that she turned her back on the genre where she found her start. Some of Jennifer's heroines wear glasses or wouldn't mind losing a few pounds, but they all have what it takes to get the guy hot and bothered. On her website the popular author makes her loyalties clear. "Trying to find something bigger and better than romance would be impossible," she writes. Also stupid, since the genre accounts for half of all mass-market paperbacks sold.

When it comes to feedback, Jennifer has experienced the gamut—"MFA feedback, Amazon feedback, editor feedback, you name it," she told me. And on top of that are the "Cherries"—an online community of readers and writers that is part Jennifer Crusie fan club, part gabfest on topics ranging from recipes to the best way to hide dead bodies, and part writing workshop—which the author relies on for critiques of her work.

In the following Q&A, Jennifer, now a *New York Times, USA Today,* and *Publishers Weekly* best-selling author of twenty novels (as well as the editor of three essay anthologies), shares her thoughts about feedback.

Do you think feedback is useful to writers?

Depends on the feedback. People who criticize pop fiction because it's not "as good" as literary fiction are like people who eat roast beef and complain it's not chicken. It's not about what's good, it's about their tastes and what they expect from a book. So that kind of feedback is pretty much worthless because they're not criticizing what you wrote, they're criticizing you for not writing what they wanted. And this is the basis for a lot of reader criticism. One reader didn't like one of my books because the heroine's best friend was gay, and that did not fit into her world of admirable women. One reviewer didn't like another book because the heroine asked the hero for time to figure out her life before she settled down. In that reviewer's story-world, women did not put relationships on hold, so the story failed for her. Clearly, these are not my story-worlds, so the fact that these readers rejected the books is inevitable. You don't take that kind of feedback personally, and you don't change your worldview. You just accept that not everybody thinks or sees the world the same way as you do, and move on.

What's your feedback process?

For professional feedback, I have a small pool of readers, including my daughter, my editor, my agent, and my long-time critique partner. The Cherries are also invaluable. A couple of them read my work when I've gotten it to the final draft stage. I don't always take their suggestions, but I always pay attention to the places they had trouble, and try to figure out what went wrong for them. If somebody says, "This section was boring" when I know it has good stuff in it, I figure I've buried the good stuff in too many words, too much dialogue, too much narrative, and I pare it down. My mantra is from Elmore Leonard: Try not to write the parts people skip.

Do you have any good "bad feedback" stories?

I got a huge packet of PETA materials once from a woman who'd read *Bet Me* and was upset because the heroine was overweight. She believed fat people get that way by being cruel to animals, so she sent me brochures and handouts, and had circled key points in marker and made notes in the margins. I never did get the connection—overweight people eat meat?—but she was adamant that I join the crusade and never write another overweight heroine again.

Some reviewers are obviously dealing with issues of their own and, if your book hits one of those, it can also result in some pretty weird evaluations. I had one reader say that *Bet Me* was too close to formula romance, then added, "Where was the dog?" and a few other things that are often in my books. As somebody else pointed out, she didn't object to formula fiction, she objected because I hadn't written the formula she liked. But most of the criticism I get from readers is honest and thoughtful, and I pay attention.

Any feedback-related advice for writers?

Here's the key thing: A story is a collaboration between a writer and a reader. If the novel is constructed with enough white space for the reader to move into it, it becomes a visceral experience for her. She writes the story with you by filling in the blanks, seeing in her mind what the characters look like, sound like, what the setting looks like, what the characters are feeling, even what they want to a certain extent, even if you've put the goals clearly on the page.

Also, feedback is absolutely critical once you've reached the "finished" stage, the point at which you have solved all the problems you can see. Then you give it to others so they can find the weak spots and you can go back in and figure out the problem. I remember doing a critique for a contest winner, a really detailed analysis of where her strengths and weaknesses were and where the story needed work. I got back an email, "LOL, Jenny, the book is finished." I wanted to write back, "LOL, in more ways than you know."

THE CLUB

I know what it feels like to be an outsider, to be a wannabe in a world where everyone else seems to belong to "The Club." I understand this sense of isolation and dejection because that is how I felt whenever I listened to *Car Talk*, a call-in show that used to be on National Public Radio and featured two Boston-based brothers who worked as mechanics and loved to whoop it up on the air about other people's car problems.

The show was on the air for thirty years and remained popular to the very end, but I just never got the appeal. All right, let's be honest here. I hated that show. Hated it! How could thousands and thousands of highly educated, upscale, influential listeners—*exactly* the kind of demographic profile in which I longed to be included—enjoy the banter of these two brothers (who went by the irritating nicknames of Click and Clack), let alone call them on the air to ask about their stuck clutches and harrumphing engines?

Ratings don't lie, however, and apparently everyone in the universe—everyone but me, that is—loved *Car Talk*, whether they drove a Ram-tough pickup, a smug Prius, or a gas-guzzling SUV for the sake of the children. At no time was I more aware of my isolation than on my family's Sunday-afternoon road trips, trapped inside our 2005 Ford Taurus (or was it a '07? as if I cared) while those two beloved, MIT-educated radio hosts entertained my yukking-it-up husband and kids as I sullenly worked my crossword puzzle.

Yes, it is a terrible thing to feel like an outsider. Yet, in the writing realm, that is how about 99.9 percent of us feel. In our heads we envision an exclusive club—The Club of *Real Writers*—to which we don't belong. At the gates to

The Club, discouraging our tentative approach, sneers a trivisage dog bearing the likenesses of Jane Austen, The seventh Duke of Wellington, and that ninth-grade teacher who failed us in English composition because we started a sentence with "And." Inside The Club, gathered around the ponderous oak tables, the Real Writers laugh hysterically over their glasses of absinthe at our miserable attempts to associate with them. "Who do you think you are?" they demand. "Where have you published?" they snicker. "Don't you make a living in sales?"

On a regular basis I hear writers talk passionately about the stories in their hearts they feel compelled to put down on paper; the sense of satisfying exhaustion they experience after a good writing session; and the drive that lures them at 4:00 a.m. to their computer table, tucked in a corner of their semifinished basement, where they struggle with that stubborn plot point before the kids wake up and the real workday begins. Yet most of these writers inevitably end the conversation by discounting their own genuineness. "Of course, I'm not a *Real Writer*," they apologize, as if they have in some way overstepped their bounds.

Why do so many people who are writing feel this way? What propaganda have we internalized that leads us to believe that practicing the craft of writing is not enough to call ourselves real? And if we are writing, but we are not Real Writers, then what are we? Are we Fake Writers? Is there even such a thing? Doesn't that suggest we are simply going through the motions, waving our fingers above the computer keys or hovering our pencils over the writing tablet but never making contact?

In the feedback process, our first challenge as writers is to stop listening to that collective chorus of naysayers who have lodged themselves between our ears and who are incessantly whispering reminders of our illegitimacy—"You are not a Real Writer . . . YOU are NOT a Real Writer . . . YOU ARE NOT A REAL WRITER!"

Here I feel obligated to warn you that if you are unpublished, if you have a life outside writing where people prefer that you simply pack lunches and earn a decent salary, or if you are even just a tad insecure, it will not be easy to shut these naysayers up. Egging them on is a culture of literary snobbism with a long history of disqualifying potential members of The Club on totally subjective criteria, including gender, race, and other bizarre factors. For example, I once read in a writing manual (by an author whose first novel I loved) that you are not a Real Writer unless you can read Horace and Livy in the original Latin. Say what?! This advice was from the same author who also felt compelled to brag that the very first book she ever checked out of the library (at age five) was Strickland's *Queens of England* (volume 1). I think this author has issues. I think perhaps she has a need to prove to her readers that she is very smart; in fact, maybe just a wee bit smarter than they are. She wants to prove she deserves to be in The Club.

Please don't misunderstand. I am not saying that learning Latin isn't a worthwhile pursuit. But what good does it do, for example, to tell a harried mom with three young kids, a job, a husband on the road half the time, and exactly five minutes to herself during normal people hours that she can't be a writer unless she manages to fit in a college course on a dead language? In a case such as this, the voice in that woman's head should be saying something like, *Latin, hmmm? Latin, oh dear. Latin, oh, shut up!*

Of course, outside forces are not the only ones at fault for making so many writers feel like inferior posers. Writers are perfectly capable of doing this sort of thing all on their own. In fact, we are the masters of trash-talking our own legitimacy. My friend Lori, who teaches fiction writing to convicted sex felons, told me about a big, scary-looking guy in her class who broke down in tears early in the term, confessing he wasn't a writer. "Why not?" Lori asked him. His reply, "I got bad handwriting."

My heart goes out to this fellow, and yours should too because, except for the sex offender part, this man is no different than you or me or all those other writers out there who harbor misguided notions about what it means to be a Real Writer. You may think, given the man's rap sheet, that the voice in a sex offender's head is a bit more perverse than most. But I can tell you, when it comes to believing in ourselves as writers, this fellow is no more misguided than most of us. I am astounded at the reasons people in my writing workshop, and people I encounter in the world at large, offer for why they are not Real Writers. Here is just a small sample of what the voices in these people's heads are telling them:

You are not a Real Writer because you don't write every day.
You are not a Real Writer because you are eighty-eight years old.
You are not a Real Writer because you have never been published.
You are not a Real Writer because you are not Rita Dove.
You are not a Real Writer because you had a happy childhood.
You are not a Real Writer because who are you to call yourself a real writer?
You are not a Real Writer because your ex-boyfriend never liked your "silly" stories.

What is the voice inside your head telling you? I hope it is not telling any lies like the ones above. Because the truth is, if you are writing you already meet the criteria for a Real Writer. You already belong to The Club. In fact, you are a lifelong member, despite any negative feedback to the contrary, because The Club of Real Writers is one club where no one—no one with stories they want to tell or a voice longing to be heard—should ever feel like an outsider. As writers, we are all better served not by creating snobby distinctions among ourselves but by fostering a sense of camaraderie.

So come inside. Make yourself at home. The Club of Real Writers welcomes one and all, and a rejection letter buys you a free drink. Published, unpublished, literary or commercial, young or old—there is room for everybody who wants to belong. Just look at all those available seats waiting to be claimed. Grab one at the table full of graphic novelists; it's fun to see what they're doodling on their napkins. Or pull up a stool next to the ghost of Thomas Hardy; he looks like he could use a good joke. Better yet, work the room, because once you start mingling you'll see that you fit in just fine—as long as you don't ask the published authors to hook you up with their agents, especially if you haven't even finished writing your second chapter.

Exercise

Write down the top ten reasons you are not a Real Writer. Note: it is very important that you put these reasons down on paper. Why? Because seeing them in black and white will show you how ridiculous they are. When you are finished, write something, anything, as long as it is from the heart.

WAITING FOR FEEDBACK

Wednesday at 10:07 a.m. you send the final revisions of your manuscript to your agent, who has agreed to shop it around to publishers. Your immediate reaction is elation. You have done it! You are magnificent! Fame and riches will soon be yours! A celebration is in order; that is, if you can find some friends who are still taking your calls after months of listening to you whine about whether you would ever finish your book.

This sense of elation lasts maybe eighteen minutes, about the time it takes for you to wash your hair for the first time in weeks and find a clean pair of sweatpants. Now comes the hard part.

Waiting.

Waiting.

Waiting.

For writers with manuscripts out to agents, editors, or other high-stakes readers, waiting for feedback—whether it represents a publisher's acceptance or approval from someone whose opinion matters to you—is not just hard; it is also a twenty-four-hour job requiring your undivided attention. When you are waiting, you must concentrate all your energy on not calling the feedback provider to "touch base." You must obsessively check email and voicemail to make sure you have not missed any messages. And if the work is out to potential publishers, you must negotiate constantly with the mercurial gods of acceptance. *If I clean the inside of my coffee machine, an offer will come through by tomorrow. If I don't eat this bag of Funyons, at least two—no, three—publishers will express interest in my work . . . If someone, oh dear God, anyone, will just agree to publish me, I will never again tell the student fundraisers from my college that I am not me,*

or abandon my discarded grocery cart in the middle of the parking lot, or roll my
eyes when someone says they need those bespoke sheets because it's all about self-care.

Embarrassingly enough, these types of behaviors reflect my own experience with waiting. I once spent seven months hoping to hear back from an editor about one of my books. I remember hitting bottom near the end of that marathon. Ever vigilant, I had checked my phone for any new emails for the umpteenth time, despite the fact it was a national holiday. The spinning icon on the screen indicated it was receiving... receiving... receiving... Maybe the editor had come in on his day off! My heart started pounding... pounding... pounding. *Oh, please be an offer! Please be an offer! Please be an offer!*

Pop! A single new message appeared in my inbox.

From: Sue
To: Joni B. Cole
Subject: Complimentary Mortgage Calculator

"Fuck-fuck-fuck-fuck-fuckingness-fuck!!!" What a memorable display *that* was for my daughter, who was six at the time and who had just happened to come into the room to ask if she could watch another episode of *SpongeBob*.

I make but one excuse for this behavior: Waiting sucks. It can suck up all our positive energy, our ability to write, and our belief in a benevolent Supreme Being. No one conveys this reality better than Samuel Beckett in his play about two tramps waiting by a tree for a man named Godot, who never arrives. As the tramps' vigil extends to a second day, allowing them time to reflect on the sorry condition of their lives, the theme of Beckett's play becomes excruciatingly clear: life is eternally hopeless and humans are absurdly insignificant. Waiting will do that to a person.

Unfortunately, no panacea exists that can make waiting for feedback from high-stakes readers any easier for writers. But I have learned through my own experience that there is something you can do to make this nerve-racking period bearable, and even enjoyable. You can stop waiting.

Stop waiting.

Stop waiting.

Stop waiting.

Or, to put it another way, you can consciously choose *not* to wait. After all, life is a series of choices about how to behave. So instead of focusing all of your energy on actively waiting to hear back from your agent or a publisher or your critique group or writing instructor or any reader, why not choose to direct it toward something affirming, something that isn't waiting? For example, you could take up origami, or paint the bedrooms tangerine, or learn how to speak Dutch. The key is to engage in something other than waiting. Change the channel. Do something, anything you like, as long as it isn't waiting.

Of course, telling yourself to stop waiting is a lot easier than actually doing it. One reason is because waiting is an automatic response; it just happens naturally, like entropy. It also feeds on itself. The more you wait, the harder it is to quit, until eventually you become so addicted to waiting that you cannot shut off your phone for even *one second* because if you do, then that will be when your agent chooses to call with big news. And if you miss that call ... or don't respond to that text immediately ... there goes your writing career!

Making it even harder to stop waiting is that most of us still engage in magical thinking. Remember when you were a kid and you thought you were the one who caused Uncle Jerome's car accident because the last time he visited your parents you kept wishing he would just go away and leave you and your Barbies the hell alone? Well, all these adult-years later, most of us still believe that if we think about something hard enough—actively wishing for that job offer to come through or that man to call or that publisher to say yes—we can actually *control* the outcome.

Of course, that is not how the universe works. In fact, my suspicion is that the universe resents, in particular, writers who think they have a modicum of control over their submissions once they send them out. That is why it holds out on us, purposely refusing to give us what we want when we want it. But if we concede our powerlessness, if we accept that the future of our manuscript is out of our hands, then that is when the universe just might drop an acceptance in our laps. Plop. Have a nice day.

During the seven months I drove myself crazy waiting to hear from the editor who was considering my book, my friends gently tried to teach me this lesson. "Move on," they suggested. "Let it go," they counseled. "Give it up to the universe," they advised. At the time, these friends really got on my nerves. Hell-bent on waiting, I was completely incapable of registering my car, let alone the deeper truths of their metaphoric wisdom. Give it up to the universe? What was that but a bunch of la-la language, a New Age-y way of saying, "Give up, you loser, that manuscript of yours will never reach publication."

One day when I was on the computer, once again waiting for an email from the editor that did not arrive, I happened upon an interview with rock bass pioneer Jack Casady, one of the founders of Jefferson Airplane. Casady was talking about "rests," the spaces between the notes, and how they are as important as the notes themselves. Without rests you don't have music, you have noise. Casady pointed out that a lot of musicians get nervous coming in after rests, so they tend to play a lot of notes to plug in the holes.

Reading this article, it occurred to me that I was doing the same thing: plugging in the holes of my day with waiting simply because I was nervous about what came next. Exhausted from so many months of relentless waiting, this notion of rest, more tangible to me than letting go or giving something up to the universe, felt like a doable, comforting alternative. I also loved what Casady said about rests helping the artist cultivate groove. It's not just about playing the same lick over and over, he said; the spaces in the music have to groove as well as the notes. Goodness knows, I needed to get my groove back, so I decided to stop filling in the spaces of my day with so much noisy waiting. I decided to give waiting a rest.

Rest.

Rest.

Rest.

For me, resting didn't come as naturally as waiting. I had to struggle to resist the impulse to jump into the empty spaces of the day and check my email. I had to stop myself from repeating the same licks over and over—*Oh, please make an offer! Please make an offer! Please make an offer!* I had to work hard to give waiting a rest.

Eventually, however, the more I stopped waiting the better I felt, and in those interludes of rest I discovered something truly worthy of my attention: the present, the here and now. And, my goodness, who should I see there but my two adorable children! My, how they had grown over those past seven months. And look! There, out my window, a tree was sprouting buds and reso- nating with birdsong. Could it really be springtime already? And halloo! Who belongs to that voice, the one calling out to me in my head? Why, it's a creative- type person with an idea for a new book. I think I'll go to the computer and see what she's got to say . . .

And so I began writing again, something I hadn't been able to do pro- ductively for months. Freed from the exhaustion of waiting for a publisher and obsessing about whether someone else thought my work was good enough, I actually remembered why I liked writing in the first place. And the funny thing is, I became so consumed with my new project, writing for the sake of writing rather than for someone else's approval, that when my phone finally did ring a few weeks later, I decided to let it go to voicemail. Because when you are writing instead of waiting, the universe can just leave a message.

ARCHER MAYOR:
"EMOTION IS A BLINDING FORCE."

I'm on the phone interviewing Archer Mayor, author of an acclaimed series of thirty-three police-procedural novels, when he gets another call and puts me on hold. After he comes back on the line, Archer offers a quick apology and explains that the caller was one of his medical-examiner colleagues. He wanted to give Archer a heads-up that there had been a car accident with multiple fatalities. As back-up medical examiner for the week, Archer might be needed to provide an extra hand.

"So, where were we?" Archer then asks me pleasantly, but I'm still trying to process the shock of the car crash.

"Geez, that's just awful news," I say, taking a moment to regroup.

"It is for somebody," Archer agrees.

Archer Mayor is many things—warm, funny, gracious—but as he readily admits, "I'm not an emotional guy." In addition to being the author of the long-running series of mystery novels featuring the decent, dependable Lt. Joe Gunther of the Brattleboro, Vermont, police department, Archer also has worked as a part-time police officer, an EMT, a volunteer firefighter, and—as I was just reminded—an assistant medical examiner. "I do all those things every day," Archer explains. "That's the world I inhabit, so I take things in stride."

It's a pretty safe bet that a man who can keep his cool during emergencies, crimes, and fires probably isn't the type of author who is going to be fazed by negative feedback. "In a real-world context," Archer says, "the recommendations of some editor aren't worth getting all excited about. I think you should take your work seriously," he adds, "but not take people's responses to it equally seriously. I preach this because so many writers get upset about feedback, but I don't see the value of getting yourself all twisted up. You'll only lose the clarity of the creative vision that got you writing in the first place."

Has the popular novelist always been so level-headed about feedback? How about before he achieved the sanctity of bankable-author status, before his mystery series became a regular on the "ten best" yearly lists of the *New York Times,* the *Washington Post,* the *Los Angeles Times,* and the *New Yorker.*

"I've had a lot of interactions with a lot of editors and have never taken their words, which were sometimes harsh in the early days, to heart," says Archer. "I've understood they're just doing their job. And my job is to put aside emotion and apply a rational, thoughtful response," he adds. "Their words of advice are valuable, but I have to filter them through my own discretion because I'm the guy writing the book. I'm the guy from whose gut the book was born. So I see all recommendations as uplifting, even when I think of them as absurd."

Archer published his first Joe Gunther novel in 1988, and he has added a new book to the series about once a year. He describes his relationship with his first editor at Putnam: "Roger was terrific because he immersed himself in my manuscript. He covered it in red ink. He wasn't a very good writer, but he would rewrite passages and I'd read them and say, 'Good God, Roger, get a grip!' Then I'd throw the manuscript across the room, but immediately think, *No, this is just how he feels.* So I'd pick up the manuscript and wade through it some more. About 50 percent of his comments were very good."

So good, in fact, that even after Archer left Putnam he hired Roger as a private editor on the next several Gunther novels—a strategy he recommends for every writer. "If you only rely on one editor," Archer says, "you're shooting yourself in the foot."

Archer clarifies that his manuscript-tossing was about passion, not emotion. "Passion is a creative force," he says. "Emotion is a blinding force." The writer's relationship with an editor is a business relationship, he stresses. It shouldn't be any more emotionally charged than any other business interaction you have during the day. "If it is," he cautions, "you should work on it, because if you get all emotional and lose control, the other guy will be looking at you, wondering why you are foaming at the mouth, and you'll lose the battle."

Archer continues on a more personal note. "I had a complex childhood, and I trained myself rather constructively to ascribe value to every situation I entered, separating the reality from what we sometimes do with it in moments of explosive emotion. But the one thing I didn't want to do was become a cold, aloof person. If you're going to be a writer, you have to be an observer and feel the heat. You need to be cognizant of the emotions of a situation, otherwise you'll write in a way that approximates taking a shower in a raincoat. In my books, I don't do blood and guts, but I sure as hell do loss and pain and bereavement. And to do that you can't turn into a stone. I'm a very passionate guy," Archer says evenly, "but I titrate."

Archer Mayor

FIFTY SHADES OF WRITING

This story starts about eight years ago, with the arrival of a much anticipated email from the publishing house where the first edition of my book—*Good Naked: How to Write More, Write Better, and Be Happier*—was in production. Wrote the marketing coordinator:

> Dear Joni,
> Attached is the final version of the cover design for *Good Naked,* which the designer has asked me to pass along to you. Please note that the white gridlines are watermarks that won't be present in the finished product . . .

Even now, years later, I get aftershocks thinking about the first time I opened the attachment and saw that cover design. There, filling my screen, was the image of a naked woman's body, full-frontal, lingering in the shadows against a smoky backdrop. She was cut off from the neck up and knees down. Against the dark backdrop, two pink circles (representing the Os in the book's title) drew the eye to the woman's breasts. Her slender fingers formed a V, framing her pubis. And just below her private parts, spread across her silken thighs, was my book's subtitle—*How to Write More, Write Better, and Be Happier.*

In summary, the proposed cover for my book—a cheerful and practical writing guide based on my decades of experience as an author and teacher— depicted a nude, headless woman, beckoning book browsers from the shadows like a back-alley sex worker.

Here, I feel compelled to state that I have nothing against back-alley sex workers. I also will concede that, yes, my writing guide has the word "naked" in its title, but so do a lot of other books, like *Naked Statistics,* which has a pie chart on its cover. So, when the designer saw the title of my manuscript, what made him think of soft porn? Why did he design a cover better suited to an entirely different type of book, say *Fifty Shades of Writing?*

I reread the email to make sure I had not misunderstood. *Final version of the cover . . . Please note that the white gridlines . . .* Could the marketing coordinator who had written this email to me be any more misguided? How could she think that a few barely perceptible gridlines on the enclosed image would be my primary concern, when there was my name—Joni B. Cole—attached to a work suggesting much more for sale than writing advice?

This story comes to mind as I think about feedback during the publishing process. In this situation, I, the author, was the one tasked with providing feedback, despite being told the cover design was "final" and despite my fear of consequences. I worried that my book was already on a tight production schedule. Could the designer refuse to make changes? If I refused his refusal, could the publisher delay my book's release, or even pull it from their list? Would I end up blacklisted from the industry, a note on my file listing me as unpleasant, uncooperative, and unwilling to do nudity?

All sorts of worries, real and irrational, cluttered my thinking. But, given the situation, I felt like I had no choice but to reject this cover wholesale. I imagined my new release displayed in the creative-writing section of my daughter's college bookstore. (And she thought I had embarrassed her in the past!) For moral support, I showed the cover to a few friends, seeking their reactions:

"Is this a joke?"

"Whoa! I thought maybe you'd been exaggerating."

"Is it me, or is that woman about to get busy with herself?"

The only positive comment about the cover came from my friend Dan. "It's not *that* bad," he shrugged. "Maybe it will sell some books."

Yeah, right, I thought, and maybe people will assume those are my silken thighs. But that doesn't make it right.

My friend Dan did make a valid point. Helping a book sell is indeed one of the main considerations when designing its cover. Depending on your publishing contract, you may not have much, or any, say in the final design, and that isn't completely unreasonable.

Few authors double as designers. Our forte is plot points, not graphic concepts. We may be too wedded to our own artistic sensibilities, right down to our favorite colors. (*That dusty rose looked so nice on my bridesmaids' dresses.*) Meanwhile, we aren't thinking about the big stuff that professional cover designers know to consider. Stuff like, What is in tune with your book's tone and audience? What is most likely to draw a browser's attention? What is on trend? Is the type readable from a distance? Is the cover going to work when it is in the form of a one-inch-high icon on Amazon?

In short, if you do have a say in the final design of your cover, just be sure to carefully weigh your tastes against the designer's eye and marketing expertise. What looks good on your wall won't necessarily look good on your cover. Also, be aware that you may not love your cover at first sight, but in the end you have to ask yourself whether you will be proud of putting it out there? Remember, people actually do judge a book by its cover, so you don't want to get in the way of having your new release make a great first impression.

You also don't want to be one of *those* authors. My friends who work in publishing have told me stories—oh, how they have told me stories. The following is just one of them. An author of a scholarly book received a cover whose image was one of her choosing, but she was so unhappy about the other elements (apparently the color of the subtitle made her "vomit") she spammed the designer, the art-production manager, the managing editor, the director of the press, and even the CFO. The one person she couldn't immediately harass was her editor, who was away at a week-long conference. The press director called the editor and told her to "rein in her author," which was no small task. In the end, almost everyone at the press stopped taking this author's calls, and while the cover issue was eventually resolved, the author chose to communicate solely with the managing editor after that point.

While much of this chapter has dealt with feedback related to your book's cover, typically this is the issue (as well as your book's interior design) where you may have the least input, depending on your contract. Almost every other step of the publishing process, however, invites two-way feedback as you work with your developmental editor, your copy editor, and the marketing team.

As noted in another chapter in this book, it is important to speak up if you truly disagree with, say, your developmental editor's suggestion to drop the first three chapters. But before you react or overreact, just keep this in mind— *My gawd, you are working with a real, live professional editor!* (And, trust me, if your real, live professional editor is bored by your opening, your readers are likely to feel the same.) Also, I would not recommend crossing your copy editor, not unless you are the kind of person who knows the past tense of the verb *forsake,* all 430 uses of the word *set,* and whether this is the correct spelling of *Kyrgyzstan.*

All this to say, don't fail to put your foot down when necessary, but also listen, really listen to the professionals. Be open to their advice, and carry that open-mindedness through every step of the publishing process, from the finalization of the manuscript, through the production of the actual book, through sales and promotion. There is feedback . . . and then there is feedback from people who make their living publishing dozens and dozens of books a year.

"Trust the process," as one of my editors once said to me. "The author-publisher relationship is not a competition. It's a partnership, a dynamic. The publisher is invested financially," she reminded me, "so they want your book to succeed in every way possible."

And here I had assumed she'd been working so hard on my manuscript simply because she was my friend.

Epilogue

In case you are curious about what happened to that naked woman on the "final" cover of my writing guide, here is the rest of the story. As soon as I saw that image, I called my editor in a state of high dudgeon. As it turns out, he shared my low opinion of the cover choice, but the designer had voted him down. "Don't sweat it for now," my editor told me. "Marketing is on your side as well." This begged the question: Who was this designer with such sway he could override both my editor and the folks in marketing?

Weeks passed. My print date drew near. Each time I checked in on my sex worker, I was told that the designer remained reluctant to remove her from my cover. As a seasoned author, I am not afraid to speak my mind, but I am also not big on ultimatums. "Replace that cover or me and my book are walking!" For me, it still feels like a miracle when a publisher accepts my work. It was unfathomable to think I would do anything to jeopardize my "forthcoming release," two words I love dropping into every conversation. But I just couldn't accept that cover. This felt bigger than a battle over design. This had the stink of misogyny.

Finally, I got word. *Fifty Shades of Writing* was no more—I would see a new cover option for *Good Naked* by the end of the day. This news came in the form of an email from the same marketing coordinator who, weeks earlier, had sent along the original design. In this message she wrote:

Dear Joni,

I'm sorry for your sleepless nights. . . . I don't know whether I should be putting this in writing, but in all my time here, I don't think I've ever been this opposed to a cover design. I'm rather ashamed that I knuckled under and sent it to you anyway, and I can only imagine how you must have felt.

Later that afternoon the designer put together an alternative with the image of a fountain pen beside a notepad, similar to the clip art used in dozens of writing-related blogs and a far cry from capturing the energy and tone of my book. In forwarding this iteration, the marketing coordinator had failed to delete the designer's email to her, which I am sure was not intended for my eyes—"See if she'll like this one," he had written, as if I were some diva with an endless list of ludicrous demands—*No, I said blue M&Ms! Not green! Not red! Blue!*

Given I felt my cover deserved more than clip art, I hired an outside graphic designer to submit a different concept. The publisher ultimately chose this cover option for my book, though I heard through the grapevine that the *Fifty Shades of Writing* designer didn't like it. (Perhaps he was distracted by the white gridlines?) So, all's well that ends well, though this story has one more chapter.

About a year after the release of *Good Naked,* the publishing house went under, which was a real blow not just because it orphaned my book, but because of all the talented and lovely people who worked at the press, and all the meaningful titles it had released to the world for almost fifty years. I was lucky to find my own happy ending, however, as *Good Naked* was picked up by a different publisher that invited me to create a second edition. Oh, and it was love at first sight when they showed me their revised version of the cover!

Now, in my better moments, when I think about that designer with whom I so fervently disagreed, I try to let bygones be bygones. I hope that he found employment at some other publishing house, assuming he is no longer living out his male fantasies on the covers of other authors' new releases. But if the challenge of my own cover struggle has taught me anything, it is this: There is good naked, and there is bad naked, but only one of those can help you write more, write better, and be happier, and it is not the one that has anything to do with soft porn.

THE VALUE OF TOXIC FEEDBACK

When I was a teenager, I obsessed about my looks to the point where my mother's refrain became, "Oh for God's sake, get away from that mirror. No one's going to be looking at you anyway." Years later, I recognized this as my first lesson in the value of toxic feedback. Someone can say something that is harsh or even unmotherly, but that doesn't mean there isn't some wisdom or benefit to be gained from the experience.

As writers, it behooves us to develop some survival techniques, or at least a little humor, when it comes to handling derogatory comments about our work. You can't be a writer and not experience toxic feedback. It goes with the territory, whether you present your writing in a critique group or on a store's bookshelf. Everybody's got an opinion.

Part of me thinks, *How sad that every feedback provider can't be sensitive and supportive when talking about a writer's work, especially given the fact that so many of us consider our words to be an extension of our souls.* But another part of me thinks, *Oh well, what the heck.* Feedback providers are only human, and we all make mistakes. I don't mean to make excuses for feedback providers who behave badly, but ultimately it is up to the writer to learn how to deal with toxic feedback—and maybe even get something positive from the experience. Think of it this way. Every day we are surrounded by toxic substances—gasoline, weed killer, nail-polish remover—that make our lives better. The same point can be made about toxic feedback. It can kill us or serve us, depending on how we use it.

Some of the people I admire most in life are those who have experienced toxic feedback and didn't let it stop them. There is the graduate student whose advisor prefaced his remarks about her dissertation on feminism in Victorian literature with the words, "I couldn't help but laugh," but she steeled herself against his condescension and completed her doctorate. There is the poet who wanted to try writing prose. "Stick to poetry," advised a member of her writing workshop, but she refused to be confined in that way. Instead she became more attuned to the lyricism in her language and how it helped or hurt each scene. There is the journalist who was once told by an editor, "You can talk, but you can't write," so he made his prose more conversational and stopped trying to sound so intellectual. And there is the timid writer who asked her husband to read a story before she gave it to her creative-writing class. "You aren't going to submit *this*?" he asked her on her way out the door. But she did submit her manuscript to the group, and in doing so learned that it is okay to show works-in-progress; the whole point of feedback is to help someone write or revise forward productively—just make sure you show your work to someone who understands the value of every draft and who has a better sense of timing.

Then there is my neighbor Pat, who works in social services, making sure housebound people receive medical care. Pat is one of my role models because she is such a good person and because I envision her as the kind of mother I might have had if I'd lived in a 1950s television show. Always nicely turned out, one time Pat came over to my house with one of those old-fashioned pink sponge curlers coiled in her hair. I knew she must have overlooked it, but I didn't tell her because seeing that curler gave me comfort—transporting me back to a safer, more innocent time.

I visited with Pat shortly after she returned from her fortieth reunion at her all-girl Catholic high school in New Jersey. Pat told me how she and her former schoolmates had reminisced about Sister Mary Martin, a formidable woman who had taught a class on poetry and was clearly a sadist. The nun specialized in ridiculing her students in front of their classmates. "I'll never forget," Pat said. "The class was talking about a poem I'd written, and Sister Mary Martin immediately shot it down, saying it was a bad idea for a poem."

Forty years ago, being respectful meant never contradicting the teacher, so Pat didn't defend her idea or stand up to Sister Mary Martin, and of course she felt the sting of the nun's public admonishment. At the same time, however, Pat had the sudden realization that this intimidating authority figure was wrong. *To hell with you,* Pat thought, which was no meaningless curse coming from a Catholic schoolgirl to a nun. "Sister Mary Martin's feedback actually got me fired up," she said. "It made me more committed to my own convictions."

One of the reasons I wanted to share Pat's story is because it shows how long hurtful criticism can resonate with a writer. Forty years is nothing in the lifespan of toxic feedback, especially when it comes from a bride of Christ. As a feedback provider, I also see this example as a cautionary tale about the repercussions of humiliating writers. When I am inclined to say something mean to a writer, maybe because I am in a bad mood or feeling jealous, or simply because I skipped lunch, I think about Sister Mary Martin all those decades ago, now cursed to an eternity in hell. What a waste of prayer and celibacy. What a reminder to be more careful with my words.

More importantly, Pat's story exemplifies how toxic feedback can benefit us in unexpected ways. I have always been struck by Pat's commitment to what she believes in; this is one of the traits I have respected most about her during our decade-long friendship. The strength of her own convictions, even in the face of formidable opposition, has served her well, particularly given her job in social services, a favorite target for state and federal budget-cutting hawks. When Pat told me the story about Sister Mary Martin, I realized that her fortitude took root forty years ago in the most unassuming of places—a poetry class in an all-girl Catholic high school. Hearing Pat's story made me understand that the value of toxic feedback isn't limited to how we apply it to writing but includes how we apply it to life. Pat could have been diminished by Sister Mary Martin's feedback. Instead she became a stronger person because of it.

As writers and as people, if we have to deal with toxic feedback then let's deal with it in a way that does us some good. Let's not allow other people's disparaging remarks to undermine our faith in our ideas or our potential. Let's use toxic feedback instead as an opportunity to reaffirm our own convictions, to show we are made of sterner stuff, and maybe even to take away a life lesson or two.

I think about my mom's comment when I was a teenager. "No one's going to be looking at you." For years I bristled whenever she made this remark, though you would have thought I'd find some comfort in the notion given that I hated my looks at the time. Eventually, however, I grew up and was able to gain some wisdom from the experience. Maybe people were looking at me; maybe they weren't. But the value of my mom's feedback came when I realized that I needed to live my life without worrying about it one way or the other.

A Clarification

After reading this chapter, I worry you might get the false impression I have something against nuns, given that nasty story I shared about Sister Mary Martin. So let me counter here with another nun story about Sister Ancilla, also an English teacher at a Catholic school, this one in South Dakota.

Sister Ancilla was the great aunt of my editor, Elise. Years ago, when Elise was in graduate school and working as a teaching assistant in a beginning poetry class, her great aunt offered this advice: "Always pull out at least one positive thing you like about the work and let the writer know." Today, as a senior acquisitions editor, Elise still puts that advice into practice, even when she rejects someone's work. (Elise also makes a point to use a pencil when editing manuscripts, to avoid the aggressive cliché of red ink.)

So, yes, as I wrote earlier in this chapter, forty years is nothing in the lifespan of toxic feedback, especially when delivered by someone in a habit. But equally enduring is the wisdom of a nun like Sister Ancilla, whose kind advice still gently guides her great niece's (and my editor's) pencil, of which I am very grateful.

JUAN MORALES:
"MY ENTRY INTO CREATIVE WRITING STARTED WITH IMPOSTER SYNDROME."

It's a feeling shared by many young writers, an insecurity that their voice or style or subject matter is nothing like that of their classmates in a workshop. But for Juan Morales, son of an Ecuadorian mother and Puerto Rican father, his status as a first-generation university student exacerbated that feeling of not belonging. "I went on a lot of detours trying to fit in," Juan says, "trying to write what I thought a workshop dictated."

Today Juan is the author of three poetry collections, including *The Handyman's Guide to End Times*, which won the International Latino Book Award in 2019. Given that this latest collection intertwines poems about zombie dating, broken souls, and the celebration of life's complexity, it's hard to imagine that this author once worried about fitting in. Yet Juan still remembers how he suffered imposter syndrome as an English major at Colorado State University Pueblo, and how one of his professors, the poet and translator David Keplinger, reassured him that he didn't need to write like everybody else. As Juan's mentor through several creative-writing classes, Keplinger advocated that the aspiring poet discover his own authentic voice. Juan shares how the professor's feedback took the form of full-on encouragement—"You can do this. You should look into a career as a writer."

For a kid raised in a family more inclined toward military service than academia, a career as a writer felt like even more of a stretch. Juan's dad grew up in Puerto Rico and had a job cutting sugarcane before he left the island to come to America, where he served in the army for thirty-one years, fought in two wars, and received two Purple Hearts. "My parents were supportive and let me kind of explore and play sports, and be a drama nerd, and do speech and debate," Juan says. "But, at the same time, there were moments during college where my dad was like, 'What can you do with an English degree?'"

Even after Juan graduated from college, his father still pushed for the pragmatism and financial security of a military career, which is how he had supported his own family and which was the route followed by Juan's brother and sister. "Juancito," his father had urged him, "now that you have a degree, you can enlist and become an officer." Several years later his father only slightly adapted his logic, telling his son, "Well, I think you're too old for the military, but you would be a good police officer."

Despite his dad's well-intentioned campaign to steer him into a more practical career, Juan resisted. His writing classes in college had only served to make him understand something he'd felt deep down, even when he was a kid: he had always been a writer. To further his own dreams, Juan attended graduate school at the University of New Mexico. It was there he worked with the poet and essayist Lisa D. Chavez, who served as his thesis advisor. In comparing Lisa to his former teacher, David Keplinger, Juan describes her as "the opposite kind of mentor." He explains, "She also was encouraging, but very challenging. Some of the best feedback she gave me was asking that question that gives you the permission and courage to dismantle an entire poem and then rebuild it."

Juan recognizes how the support and instruction he received from both of these mentors—"a mingling of positive feedback and the stern mentor"—contributed to his debut collection, *Friday and the Year that Followed*, which garnered the first of several poetry prizes. Juan shares how the book was inspired by the stories his family told while sitting around the coffee table about war, about how his mother survived an earthquake in Ecuador, about ghosts. His father has passed now, but Juan makes a point to add how his family often attended his readings or book events. "It's great to be part of a family that's supportive. It's really wonderful."

Today Juan is back at his undergrad alma mater, Colorado State University Pueblo, where he teaches and serves as the associate dean of the College of Humanities Arts and Social Sciences. (Juan smiles when he shares, "It wasn't until I was a tenured professor that my father was like, 'Okay. I think you did okay for yourself.'") Juan is also curator of the CSU-Pueblo student literary magazine, *Tempered Steel*, and the editor of the national literary magazine *Pilgrimage*. As we talked about teaching and mentoring, he made a reference to the "fundamentals of feedback," so I asked him to elaborate.

"The core of good feedback is making sure the writer gets what they need to open doors," he says. "The worst forms of feedback are no feedback and don't-change-a-thing feedback. For example, if someone says, 'Damn, that's a great story, I don't have any notes for you,' that isn't enough.

"I always like to talk about the highlights in a work," Juan continues. "The highlights are fundamental because, as writers, we often overlook what we're doing right. The writer might be thinking, *I had no idea I was good at titles,* until three members of a workshop point it out. Or they might think they have a bad idea for a manuscript until they hear differently, which then motivates them to look at how they can excavate the idea even more."

In his classes, Juan reaffirms that the relationship—whether between teacher and student, writer and editor, or workshop participants—requires communication on both fronts and asking effective questions.

"I'm all about un-silencing the workshop," Juan says, citing one example of "toxic feedback" from his own student days, when he was expected to quietly listen as workshop members discussed how one line in his poem might be better served by replacing the existing last word, "flavor," with a Spanish alternative. "Growing up in a bilingual household, there was a lot of code switching," Juan says, "so listening to a fifteen-minute discussion about my language, I just cringed and got very defensive. *What word do you want me to use?* I thought but didn't say. *Guacamole? Tortilla? Frijoles?* Without the opportunity to offer context, it felt like my cultural background was just something to add for flavor, an exotification of what I was trying to accomplish, and not what I was really trying to do."

Juan strongly advocates for a more holistic approach to the feedback interaction, to make room for the writer to understand the feedback and discover opportunities to find the humor or the wisdom in a piece and to make sure the feedback provider understands the intentions of the work. "We have to make sure people remember that the writing process can be exciting, fun, torturous, an avenue to discovery," he says. "Especially with COVID and other stressors in our lives, we have to remember that we need to have time to play on the page, whether it's prose or poetry."

"I never should have brought you to my writing workshop."

PREVENTING MENTAL MELTDOWNS

Here is a scientific fact: People can only process small amounts of information at a time before their heads implode (figuratively speaking). This reality was actually quantified in a study by cognitive-science researchers at the University of Queensland, who concluded that four is the maximum number of individual variables a person can mentally handle while trying to solve a problem. And that is on a very good day. Add just one more variable and the result is a mental meltdown. The person loses track of the information, his confidence plummets, and the odds of seeing any improvement in performance are no better than chance. This is particularly true in high-stress jobs like air-traffic control, where people must juggle multiple factors at once.

Of course, air-traffic control is a cakewalk compared to writing, where the writer has to keep track of everything from plot points and the rules of grammar to which characters cover their roots or take cream in their coffee. Because writers carry the weight of this responsibility around with them all the time, feedback providers need to restrain themselves when offering constructive criticism. It is so easy to get carried away with all the important things we have to say while failing to notice that the writer has actually fallen off her chair, eyes wobbling in their sockets from information overload. Underscoring this need for restraint is the fact that when we are giving feedback to writers (as opposed to air-traffic controllers or nonwriters), we have to take into account not only cognitive science but also abnormal psychology.

Every writer has a split personality—Creator and Editor—and these two sides of the same person have a habit of sabotaging each other's efforts. Good writers understand this, so they strive to keep a healthy distance between their

Creator and Editor during the writing process. As a feedback provider, you also need to be aware of these temperamental opposites within every writer. Otherwise, when you present your feedback you are bound to overlook the feelings of one or the needs of the other, hence undermining everybody's efforts.

The Creator is an artistic genius prone to agonizing bouts of self-doubt (when he isn't feeling completely full of himself). His job is to tap the writer's unconscious, allowing all that rich, unfiltered story material within him to flow onto the page. If the Creator thrusts his impassioned scribbling at you and suggests you peruse it on the spot while he just hangs out in the corner, the smartest thing you can do is to read expressively (here, widen your eyes in breathtaking anticipation; there, shed tears of anguish; here, laugh uproariously). This will get your relationship with the Creator off to a good start. What you don't want to do at this point is dwell on the Creator's jarring point-of-view shifts or impenetrable idiolect or the fact that he doesn't always spell the main character's name the same way. This will only block the Creator's creative flow and give him the vapors.

The Editor, on the other hand, welcomes constructive criticism because it helps him to do his job, which is to clean up the Creator's mess. (You can see why these two sides of the writer don't always get along.) The Editor is capable of achieving miracles in the revision process, but he may not be able to even start reseeing or rewriting his initial efforts if you confront him with too many problems at once. The best thing you can do for this side of the writer is to help him focus his attention. Give the Editor and yourself permission to let some of the story's faults slide until the next draft, or the next, or the next. In other words, don't worry about dangling participles until the plot hangs together.

Now that I've made it clear how cognitive science and abnormal psychology relate to writers, I'll play out an example of how they apply to the feedback process. Let's say a novelist has asked you to critique what you would call a disaster, but what is more commonly referred to as a typical first draft. Your first impulse might be to say something like, "The main character is cardboard, the plot lags, the flow of thoughts is disorganized, the setting is nondescript, there are too many summaries and not enough scenes, the climax fizzles, the writing is sloppy, I don't get the ending, and, by the way, you're ugly, too!" But that is *exactly* what I'm talking about when I warn feedback providers about how easy it is to get carried away.

A more effective strategy is to concentrate your criticism on just one or two issues. Often characterization is a good place to focus the writer's attention during the early stages of a work, since character drives plot and provides the heart of any good story. But before offering *any* constructive criticism, don't forget about the Creator's need for reassurance. It is no easy feat to sow the seeds of a character on a blank page, and this deserves to be recognized. You can also help the Creator gear up for the next draft by asking him thought-provoking questions about the protagonist, whom I'll refer to as Samantha. For example, what does Samantha want? What do her coworkers think of her? Where did she grow up? What's in her grocery cart or the drawer of her bedside table? This type of noncritical feedback helps the Creator because it stirs his creativity, prompts character development, and reminds him that it can be useful to write outside the story. Plus, it is fun for both of you to discuss Samantha as if she is a real person.

Once you have met the Creator's needs, it is time to put forth a measured amount of specific constructive criticism. If character development is your focus, you can highlight places where the protagonist's indifference ("Samantha was never fazed by anything her boss threw at her") diminishes your own emotional investment in the story. You can indicate places in the manuscript where you would like to be privy to what she is thinking ("Samantha stared out the window, deep in thought"). You can talk about how abstractions or generalities ("Samantha behaved inappropriately at times") are not nearly as effective as concrete details that enable you to form your own judgments about the character. And you can celebrate examples of successful characterization already evident in the manuscript ("Samantha propped her size ten Easy Striders on her boss's desk"). This last effort will show the Editor that he has already got some momentum, and that you are not asking for the impossible.

In the example I just provided, the feedback focused on the issue of characterization, but in another piece of writing a better focus might be point of view, or structure, or language. Even if the writer attends to just one issue per rewrite, he is likely to improve other aspects of the work in the process. For instance, if the writer clarifies what Samantha wants (a fresh start? power? peace of mind?), this will energize the plot as she strives to obtain her goal. If he develops the details of Samantha's life (she lives in a thin-walled unit of a condominium complex for singles; her father is a retired army colonel who still barks orders at everyone he meets), these enhancements will establish setting and a fictional universe. And when the writer lets Samantha act and talk and think on the page, this will transform dry summaries into powerful scenes.

Generally speaking, the rougher the draft, the fewer the variables you throw at the writer at once. In contrast, if you are critiquing a work that is in fairly good shape (hence the complexity of the challenge has been reduced), you can increase the amount of variables you include in your feedback. At that point, the writer is secure enough about his work, or practiced enough in the feedback process, that he will automatically use his own problem-solving skills to break down the criticism into small, manageable "chunks." For example, the writer may look at your dozens of notations in the margins and instinctively group them all within one variable—line edits—so as not to overtax the limits of his processing capacity.

As a feedback provider, neither you nor the writer should expect a piece to metamorphosize from an early to a final draft all in one giant honking rewrite. As such, one of your most important jobs is to meet every draft where it is at. This will help you focus your constructive advice on the one or two issues that will simply help the writer along to the next draft.

On a similar note, it's important to size your constructive criticism according to each writer's ability to digest it. Some writers can choke on a crumb; others are able to handle more feedback at one sitting, although these writers, too, need help setting priorities. I think of an accomplished writer I know working on a novel about Norwegian partisans during World War II. She once spent weeks researching the history of saunas after a feedback provider pointed out a slight inaccuracy in her text. Attention to authenticating detail is crucial in any book, especially historical fiction, but as this writer pointed out herself, perhaps not so much so when you haven't even drafted chapter 3. It is remarkably easy for writers to get bogged down or sidetracked by the millions of little things that demand their attention, but so many of these will simply have to wait their turn.

How much criticism you put forth, and how much you reserve for the next draft; what matters now and what can be addressed later: these are assessments you will want to make writer by writer and draft by draft, every time you sit down to give someone feedback. It helps to think of giving feedback not just as an art but also as a science in which cognitive researchers have proven that less is more. Giving good feedback isn't just about what you have to say; it is about what *both* sides of the writer can hear.

THE POWER OF POSITIVE FEEDBACK

January 19

Dear Mrs. Cole,

I am writing to let you know how much I disagree with you and your sunny-minded colleagues about the power of positive feedback. Today's classrooms and bookshelves are filled with bad writing. Bad, bad, bad. Writing is a discipline. At the end of the day, the job has to be done and done right. Therefore, I fail to see how coddling writers serves to expunge bad writing habits or promote excellence.

Sincerely,
Laurence Pierce, Doctoral Candidate (ABD), English Literature Chair, Committee for General Excellence

February 2

Dear Mr. Pierce,

I appreciate a man of your stature (Chair!) taking the time to write. Your point is well taken. It serves no purpose to coddle writers who need to understand that writing is rewriting and hard work, indeed. Ah, but that is why positive feedback is crucial! To borrow from the wisdom of Lao Tzu, the journey of a thousand rewrites starts with a single step. Consider the acknowledgment in a novel published by one of my former students—"To those of you who said it was good from the start, your comments were invaluable. Without someone saying that, I never would have had the courage to work on it again."

Sincerely,
Joni

P.S. Please feel free to address me by my first name. "Mrs. Cole" is better suited for my mother-in-law.

March 11

Dear "Joni,"
First, thank you for your nod to my "stature." In truth, all my life I have felt a bit underappreciated; an inevitability, I suppose, as a middle child and now as a devoted scholar of the metaphysical poet William Mauck, whose works have been largely obscured by the looming shadow of Donne. (I'll admit, at times, this goads.) Nevertheless, my views about the so-called power of positive feedback remain unchanged. When it comes to achieving excellence in writing, what practical purpose does it serve?

Sincerely,
"Laurence"

P.S. I don't suppose you have read Mauck by any chance? He is the subject of my dissertation.

April 3

Dear Laurence,
Again, you raise an important issue. The biggest fear among writers is that they have nothing of value to say. Positive feedback is the most *practical* way to overcome this fear. It motivates the writer to keep writing, and in this way he discovers his own voice and connects with his subject matter in a way that is uniquely his. Voice and passion— the heart and soul of powerful writing!

Let me give you an example of our process. Today, my workshop went on a quest—a quest to find the best aspects of a story submission (this being one of the most practical purposes of a writing workshop).

You should have been there, Laurence, to witness the collective enthusiasm. "Look here, this is amusing!" "Here, a terrific intensity of feeling!" "There, a lovely example of show, don't tell!" We've never had such a good time in the group, and the writer, an insecure, middle-aged man who brought a teddy bear to the meeting, left the class humming.

Sincerely,
Joni

P.S. I am sorry to say I have never read (or heard of) your poet, Mauck. Are you willing to send along a draft of your dissertation? I hope so!

April 17

Dear Joni,
Enclosed is a draft of my dissertation on Mauck. I must confess, I have not looked at it since receiving my advisor's initial feedback two years ago. Somewhat in my defense, the demands on me as Chair of the Committee on Excellence have consumed much of my time. Still, while I have continued my research on Mauck, I have been floundering over how to address my advisor's multitude of criticisms. I am leaning toward burning this draft, but hesitate since it represents seven years' labor.

As to the issue of positive feedback, while I concede that encouragement has its place (I recall from my research that the more-established Mauck praised the younger Donne's early efforts during their lone recorded encounter in Cambridge in 1609), I remain firm that feedback must focus on a work's deficits.

Sincerely,
Laurence

P.S. Please don't bother remarking on my dissertation. Your positive feedback is lost on me.

May 19

Dear Laurence,
Out of respect for your views, I won't offer a peep of positive feedback about your dissertation. But I assume you won't mind if I

comment on your subject. Mauck is fascinating! I found your brief mention of his use of extravagant paradox (the secular and the divine; the agony and ecstasy) particularly compelling. How he uses this technique to shock and excite his readers strikes me as the heart of your work. More!

In response to your firm stance on feedback: If the writer is only made aware of the deficits of his text, how is he to know what aspects are succeeding? You might think that writers would assume that the elements of the piece that are *not* criticized are working just fine, but writers being writers, that is rarely the case. Without the feedback provider delineating what works and why, the writer is just as likely to revise the good with the bad. A focus on the positive helps him recognize what to preserve and what to develop—two crucial steps forward *toward excellence!*

Sincerely,
Joni

P.S. Are you a father, Laurence? You seem like a wonderful role model.

August 6

Dear Joni,

Forgive my long lapse in replying to your last note. Finally, progress on my dissertation! I have enclosed a revised draft (in response to your request for "More!"). As this draft reflects, I have focused the text more on Mauck's use of extravagant paradox to shock and excite his readers. It struck me recently that this was the core of his genius. Something in my advisor's response from two years ago must have triggered this long-delayed epiphany. I shall thank him when we meet in two weeks to review this latest draft.

Sincerely,
Laurence

P.S. Regrettably, I am neither a father nor married. My former girlfriend ended our relationship two years ago on the eve of my forty-first birthday. She said I was "bringing her down."

August 18

Dear Laurence,

I was thrilled to read your revised dissertation! What is left, but polishing this diamond?

Happy news on my end, as well. Today the workshop discussed a revision of the teddy bear fellow's story. What an improvement from when we last saw it. As you may recall, our initial discussion of the work focused only on its promising aspects. Yet, with this revision, he has managed to address many of the story's deficits without benefit of our critical remarks. How did this happen, do you suppose? A stroke of luck? Or perhaps the power of positive feedback works in mysterious ways. The writer intends to continue to revise.

Sincerely,
Joni

P.S. I was sorry to read about your girlfriend's rejection (ouch!), but I have confidence that the right woman will come along.

August 30

Dear Joni,

Alas. I met briefly with my advisor regarding my revised dissertation. I struggle with how to interpret one of his comments in particular. ("Laurence, you have a small talent for scholarship.") While only one other contemporary academic has published a brief study of Mauck, I fear his will remain the definitive work, as I seem to be, once again, at a standstill.

Sincerely,
Laurence (Forever ABD)

September 12

Dear Laurence,

Don't interpret your advisor's words as a judgment, but as a challenge. Recall your own assertion about Mauck's ostracism from the Catholic church—how it only served to fuel his passion. Your research is formidable. Your focus on Mauck's use of extravagant paradox, inspired. You are connected to your subject in ways that transcend scholarship. Let your advisor's questionable comment fuel your own passion. You know Mauck deserves to be recognized as Donne's equal. Shrug off self-doubt and champion *your* Mauck!

Sincerely,
Joni

P.S. "Forever ABD . . . " Puh-leeze!

January 26

Dear Joni,
Oh happy day! Enclosed is an inscribed copy of my finished dissertation: "The Mark of Mauck: An Expression of Religious Passion through Extravagant Imagery." Despite the steepened pitch of my advisor's eyebrows when he signed off on the text (the man is as intimidating as he is learned), I felt compelled to thank him for his counsel all these many years. I could not have accomplished this work without his critical feedback.

My oral examination is in three weeks. Perhaps I should bring a teddy bear to my defense? (tee hee)

Sincerely,
Larry

P.S. I resigned my position as Chair of the Committee on Excellence. Too much on my plate. I have met a woman named Jasmine, an assistant professor of Romance languages. We see each other every Wednesday evening!

February 8

Dear Larry,
Congratulations on completing your dissertation, and on your budding romance with a professor of Romance. How poetic!

I truly value my copy of your dissertation, and particularly appreciate the inscription, "Lo, how the weary friends / View excellence through different lens." (Yes, I recognized the wordplay on the first two lines of Mauck's *The Divine*.) You don't need me to wish you luck during your oral exam. The air is already charged with positive energy and that, too (prepare yourself, Laurence, because here I go again), plays a significant role in achieving excellence.

Sincerely,
Joni

March 11

Dear Joni,
I passed! I am free of the stigma of ABD. Now I must dash to an appointment (I am getting my first salon haircut!), but I wanted to make a point to let you know, while it appears we must agree to disagree on the power of positive feedback, I respect your instincts to be gentle with that poor teddy-bear fellow in your workshop. Some people are too sensitive to be writers.

Sincerely,
Larry

April 1

Dear *Dr.* Pierce!
Congratulations on completing your Ph.D.! I am so happy for you. In celebration of your success, I have enclosed a small graduation gift, which I have named "Workshop Bear." Even as we "agree to disagree," I send this fuzzy fellow along as a reminder of the power of positive feedback. May he inspire your future writing.

Sincerely,
Joni

P.S. No need to be concerned about the "poor teddy-bear fellow" in my workshop. He finished his short story and submitted it to the *New Yorker*. You can read it in the upcoming fiction issue.

GRACE PALEY:
"MY NATURE WASN'T
AMBITIOUS ENOUGH TO
GO AHEAD ON MY OWN."

When I met Grace Paley, one of America's greatest short-story writers, in a busy café, I saw firsthand how her trademark mix of candor and affection permeates her conversation as well as her fiction. When the waitress delivered our coffees, Grace told her directly, "I hate the sandwiches here." Then she patted the young woman's arm, adding kindly, "but don't take that personally, dear."

Grace started writing short stories in the mid-1950s. At the time, she felt they were probably "trivial, stupid, boring, domestic, and not interesting," especially in a period dominated by traditionally masculine literature. Still, these were the stories that were "bugging her"; these were the people she was curious about, mostly Jewish women and mothers living everyday lives in the Bronx. Over half a century later, Grace's "trivial" stories—animated by the author's inimitable, and often comic, voice—continue to resonate with contemporary readers, writers, and teachers of writing. (And on a personal note, when I read *An Interest in Life,* the first line of that story—"My husband gave me a broom one Christmas. This wasn't right. No one can tell me it was meant kindly."—changed my life as a writer.)

Doubleday published Grace's first story collection, *The Little Disturbances of Man,* in 1959 to glowing reviews. She followed her successful debut with two more volumes of short stories, but she was not in any hurry. *Enormous Changes at the Last Minute* (1975) and *Later the Same Day* (1985) were both published by Farrar, Straus & Giroux. Grace also has published books of poetry (as a young woman, she studied with W. H. Auden at the New School for Social Research in New York), and her *Collected Stories* was nominated for the

National Book Award in 1994. Then there is the aptly titled *Just as I Thought*, a collection of her articles, reports, and talks representing about thirty years of political and literary activity.

A longtime antiwar and antinuclear protestor, a feminist, and a doting grandmother (during our conversation, Grace automatically reached for her purse to show me photos before realizing she had left it in the car), she always managed to combine the political and the personal in her writing, her activism, and her everyday life. At age eighty-three, she remained an icon of American literature and a likable "troublemaker," though when I phoned her for this interview, less than a year before her passing, she wasn't writing anything. Not because of any waning curiosity or commitment, but because her granddaughter was visiting and her typewriter was in the repair shop.

What is the role of feedback in writing?

It's either encouragement or discouragement. When I first began to write I was working alone. I sent stories out again and again to magazines, and they always came back. Many of these are the same stories that have now been anthologized. I was very discouraged. I was very discourage-able. By accident, my first three stories were read by the father of the kids I was babysitting. He was an editor at Doubleday [Kenneth McCormick, editor in chief at Doubleday from 1942 to 1971], and he told me to write seven more. If Ken hadn't said, "I'm going to publish the book," I would have continued to write, but maybe just two or three more stories, or maybe I would have gone back to writing poems, or maybe I would have had more kids. I didn't have the drive. My nature wasn't ambitious enough to go ahead on my own. I'm aware of that encouragement that people like me need.

As a short story writer focused on the lives of "ordinary" women, were you surprised by your book's success?

What I didn't know was that a very big movement was beginning— the women's movement. Every movement requires a literature, so little by little, books like mine and Tillie Olsen's ["Tell Me a Riddle," which won the O'Henry Award in 1961 for best short story] caught on. Philip Roth's first book [*Goodbye, Columbus,* a novella and five stories] also came out the same year as mine. We were all told a lot not to write short stories, to write novels instead. I wasted two or three years trying to do that. Philip, of course, did go on to write great novels, but Tillie and I just screwed around with more short stories.

Is feedback useful in learning to write?

Good literature is the best feedback you can get. You read the great stories, and what you read integrates into your language. It teaches you again and again how to write. There were a lot of short story writers I liked as a teenager. James Joyce was very important to me, not just for his short stories. In my generation we used to walk around reading *Ulysses* aloud. I also learned from reading stories by Stephen Crane. This was pre-Hemingway stuff, but I never liked Hemingway very much anyway.

You taught at Sarah Lawrence for twenty-two years. How do you help students handle criticism in the classroom?

That's a big problem. You get ten or fifteen people in a class, each with a different opinion, so you have to assert yourself as the teacher. And sometimes you get people who are destructive. That's really hard. They have to tell the truth, but it's horrible when they're right. Sometimes they might say something correct, but they're usually not, because the job of criticism is not to say how badly you've written this, but how you can write it better. I always told my students, "The point is not for anybody to kill anybody, but to be truthful, so see if you can get it together."

How do you use feedback when you write?

I take certain people's criticism seriously—my husband's and my daughter's—but I do the revising on my own. You have to learn how to do it on your own because the point of revision is to get closer and closer to what you want to say. You look at it and say, *It's nice, but that's not what I want to say.* You bring it closer and closer to your truth. So in the end, there is no help with that from anyone in the whole world.

You once wrote, "As far as the artist is concerned, all the critic can ever do is make him or break him." Does feedback from readers influence your writing?

No. Well, that's a lie. You have to fight excessive praise and excessive criticism. I get a lot of nice letters. I have to think, *I'm glad you like it, now leave me alone.* And a lot of people don't agree with me. *Commentary Magazine,* for example [a monthly magazine that takes a special interest in Jewish issues], dislikes my politics and my stories. They hate my position on things, and their literary people go after me. It's good for me, though; good for the soul to get whacked around a few times.

A RIGHT WAY AND A WRONG WAY

Some examples of the wrong way to give feedback are so blatantly wrong they need no explanation. Years ago an advertising-executive friend of mine was working at a large insurance company. He took a draft of his first writing project to his boss, the head of creative services. She tore the ten pages in half without even looking at them, then fed the ripped document into the shredder. My friend's jaw dropped. His boss asked, "Did you make a copy?" He hadn't. "Well," she said, "you have just learned two things. One, always make a copy. Two, don't attach your ego to your work."

It's easy to tell feedback providers, "Don't feed someone's work into the shredder," but what about all the other wrong ways to give feedback that have more to do with how you say something, or when you say something, or how many times you repeat the same damn thing over and over again? In giving feedback, style matters almost as much as substance. Think of your relationship with the writer as a marriage. You know that if you don't like your partner's tone of voice, you are a lot less inclined to remove your dripping pantyhose from the shower rod or lower the toilet seat, even when asked for the hundredth time. That's exactly the type of resistance you're likely to provoke in a writer if you present your feedback in the wrong way.

One of the most common wrong ways to give feedback is to deliver it in what I would call a "tsk-tsk" tone. This tone of voice sounds like it should come with a starched, white blouse over a big bosom and a blackboard with squeaky chalk. Listen for the tsk-tsk tone in the following feedback: "Well [read: *Miss Thinks She Wants to Be a Writer*], if you expect me to believe that your narrator actually works as a waitress in a casino in Atlantic City, then you really need to do your homework beforehand." Yech. I can't even stand to write that tone because now I hear it in my head—condescending and reproachful, as if the writer should have known better than to misbehave on the page.

Our job as instructors (and here I am referring to everyone who gives feedback, because all of our comments should be instructive) is to make the writer feel safe sharing works-in-progress, not like some fifth grader who just shot a spitball in class. I appreciate the following funny-not-funny story from my friend and fellow writing teacher Ed about a nonfiction-writing class he took in graduate school. He told me about how the professor's nasty proclamations ("Let's be honest here, this is boring.") proved more a distraction than help. "When everyone is uncomfortable, it's hard to take away anything meaningful," Ed shared. "As an instructor," he added, "I'm always looking around the room, reading body language. A tilt of the head or body indicates interest, but I remember in that class, everyone was sitting up straight, afraid of who was going to 'get it' next, and a lot of the time it was me." (Yes, Ed was the target of the professor's "Let's be honest . . ." comment.)

With Ed's story in mind, let's consider a few of the more effective ways that other instructor with the squeaky-chalk voice could package her thought about the characterization, without resorting to those superior-sounding "need to's" and "should's."

How about gentler phrasing: "Wow, I love the idea of your narrator being a waitress in an Atlantic City casino, but you might consider fleshing her out with more details so I can really see her."

Or how about a supportive approach: "Related to that character, the waitress in Atlantic City. I have a cousin who works at a casino. If you want, I can give you her number so you can ask her what it's like."

Or how about a strategy of "genuine ignorance," which encourages the writer to talk about the issue: "It's great you're willing to write about a character so far removed from your own experience. How are you planning to research her?" By encouraging the writer to be the educator, this creates a more dynamic interaction and an opportunity for you to gracefully insert some helpful suggestions.

Another common wrong way to give feedback is a tactic I call the "feedback filibuster." This is when the critiquer arrives at the feedback session with an agenda: to hold the floor until he convinces the writer he is right, and to deny anyone else the chance to present an alternative perspective (as in a workshop or classroom setting). The feedback provider usually starts his filibuster by reciting from a long list of all the things wrong with the draft. "Item one, improbable plot . . . Item two, stilted dialogue . . . Item twenty-seven, split infinitives . . ." As he goes on and on, rambling and riffling, he may even toss in a few positive remarks, but after a certain point it really doesn't matter because nobody is paying any attention anyway.

Rather than resorting to a feedback filibuster, a much more effective tactic is to present your comments one at a time, allowing space between each of your points for the writer to process the information or for others to follow up with their own insights about the issue. For instance, when the conversation is focused on the story's plot, that is the appropriate time to introduce your feedback about its improbability. When (and if) the story discussion segues to wordsmithing, that is a good opportunity to take issue with split infinitives. By critiquing a manuscript issue by issue, and by linking every comment to specific examples in the manuscript, you will achieve a much more coherent, interactive discussion.

As a feedback provider, you also want to tune in to "teachable moments." These are opportunities that present themselves in the course of a discussion and provide the perfect occasion to educate the writer about something that is relevant in the moment. On a fifth grade field trip to a farm, for example, when Johnny is being chased by a bull, the teacher might take that opportunity to educate the class about safety around animals. In a workshop discussion, teachable moments happen all the time. "Look everybody! See how the writer made this beautiful transition from generalized to specific time. Let's talk about transitions and why this one works so successfully."

Good feedback providers not only respond to teachable moments, they also create them by inviting the writer's thoughts at the most opportune times. "What were you intending to get across with your ending?" "How would you describe your protagonist?" "Tell me where you're heading with your plot." "What do you think are the strongest features of your prose?" "What do you think your essay is really about?"

Teachable moments are about reciprocity—the feedback provider and the writer feed off each other in a stimulating way. The flow of the discussion may not adhere precisely to a rigid agenda, but teachable moments allow you to evoke insights from the writer even while sharing your own insights, and they present the perfect opportunities to explain a narrative technique right when the writer is most open to absorbing the information.

Red-penning every single instance of a recurring weakness in the text is also a wrong way to give feedback. This is likely to leave the writer feeling queasy when he sees the bloodbath you have made of her manuscript, and it makes you come across as overbearing. A better strategy is to point out the weak pattern in the writing, highlight a few examples, and then allow the writer to take care of the rest on their own. Related to this issue is counting how many times a writer repeats a bad habit, as in, "I counted seventy-nine passive verbs in this chapter." And to make matters worse, counters are usually repeaters. "Seventy-nine passive verbs! You used passive verbs in seventy-nine sentences in this chapter alone. That's seventy-nine sentences that didn't have action verbs. I know because I counted them." Taking the time to count the flaws in another writer's manuscript could suggest a certain sadistic pleasure on the critiquer's part. It also raises the question: Doesn't the feedback provider have a life?

Let's see ... What are some other wrong ways to give feedback? It's wrong to be brutally honest when you give feedback, because any kind of brutality is just an excuse to take out your own failures on somebody else. It's wrong to criticize the writer instead of the writing, as in, "You stink at writing plots," or, "You don't have enough life experience to be a writer." It's wrong to make dismissive pronouncements: "Nobody's going to read a poem about a housewife in Newark." And here is an example of the wrong way to give feedback that is not only wrong, but ridiculous. A writer in an advanced fiction-writing class turned in a short story about a hairdresser. Her professor asked, "Have you ever been a hairdresser?" The writer answered no. "Then don't write about hairdressers," he told her.

I am sure there are lots of other wrong ways to give feedback, but this chapter is putting me in a bad mood. Plus, it reminds me of my own recent blunder, when I told a writer her characters all seemed like they belonged in a Folger's commercial. So I will close with one more example, which I hope serves as inspiration for all feedback providers to curb any obnoxious tendencies that might undermine their efforts.

A writer submitted a short story for review to my workshop. A new member of the group launched the discussion, reciting from her three handwritten pages of notes. (God bless her, because I'm sure she meant well.) Her tone was strident as she ticked off the story's offenses, though she occasionally inserted a token compliment, which only made things worse. The more the feedback provider talked, the more worked up she got, until her voice sounded like Minnie Mouse on helium. The other members of the workshop must have been stunned into silence, because no one volunteered a supporting or conflicting opinion. As the workshop leader, I knew it was my job to say or do something to stop the barrage, but frankly I was in over my head.

Finally the story discussion ended, and everyone, including Minnie Mouse, returned their written critiques to the writer. After the group disbanded and I had washed down three Advils with some pinot grigio, I thought about how well the writer had held up under the attack. She had listened attentively, a receptive expression molded on her face. Because she had been in several of my previous workshops, I knew she was thick-skinned and good at processing feedback. Once, she had even told the group that she saves her rejections from literary magazines, which I realize can be useful, but for wimps like me this seems like a form of self-flagellation.

This writer will know what to do with Minnie Mouse's feedback, I reassured myself, tossing the used coffee filter into the trash. And that's when I saw it: the discarded critique—three stapled pages of strident handwriting—dumped in the garbage and now dripping with grinds.

An Apology

Earlier in this chapter I was a bit harsh on "counters," those readers-slash-statisticians who tally the missteps in your manuscript and then confront you with categorical data. Likely we all know someone who is so myopic or math-obsessed in their critiques that they overlook more pressing issues of craft or, worse yet, fail to appreciate the overall lyricism or gravitas of our work.

I realize now, however, that counters also have a valued place in the world of feedback. This awareness became clear during my recent conversation with an author too famous to identify here, lest you think I am a shameless name dropper. But when I asked him to share an example of particularly useful feedback from his own writing life, he quickly responded, "I have this friend who counts things in my stories . . ."

The author went on to explain that sometimes this friendly counter noticed thematic repetitions, like how many times water reappeared in the manuscript, which helped to reveal patterns of which the author might or might not have been aware. Other times the friend focused on stylistic issues, like the number of sentences that started with a similar type of clause or the same pronoun.

This author's appreciation for his fastidious friend opened my eyes to my own shortsightedness. Thus, I want to apologize here and for the record to all those counters out there toward whom I might have rolled my eyes. Yes, it can be annoying as heck when you quantify our shortcomings on the page, but, on the other hand, we writers should be grateful for your diligence because, well, because twelve consecutive sentences that start with "I" is likely about ten sentences too many.

CAN YOU PLEASE BE MORE SPECIFIC!

In general, speaking in generalities has a place in communication, but it also has its limitations. For one thing, it can make people zone out (like you probably did when reading that previous sentence). This is why general information rarely makes it into our long-term memory. In addition, speaking in generalities can make you sound evasive, like when a politician says, "I promise to cut taxes!" but then fails to mention that he plans to do this by slashing federal programs that offer health insurance, housing and energy subsidies, and food, education, and childcare assistance for those most in need.

Of course, even when we aren't trying to be evasive, our generalized comments can leave others feeling nonplussed or wishing for . . . more. This was the experience of Beth Rider, a seasoned pediatrician and educator at Boston Children's Hospital and Harvard Medical School. Beth also teaches communication skills, working with faculty and medical students who seem to have no issues with peering into open chest cavities or sewing up gaping wounds but often react squeamishly to the idea of giving each other feedback.

Beth told me a story from her own student days as a pediatric resident treating inpatients at a Boston hospital. When the time came for her formal evaluation by the attending physician, the two met at the elevator en route to the sixth floor. "You're doing a great job," Beth's boss told her on the ride up. She looked forward to their conference and hearing more. Then the elevator doors opened, and he took off. End of evaluation. "It was great I got my A," Beth said, "but how did I get it? What did I do right?"

In her workshops for the medical school faculty, Beth emphasizes that good feedback is more than a grade or an evaluation. Feedback should be descriptive. The teacher should include examples that illuminate what the medical students are doing right or wrong so that they can improve performance. For instance, instead of calling an intern "lazy," which is a criticism of the student, the more useful feedback would be to direct the criticism to the behavior—"In your last workups, I noticed you took shortcuts that saved time and energy but caused you to miss the giant growth on the patient's forehead." Now that is specific feedback the student can act on.

Beth adds that the same principles of good feedback apply to the four-year-olds she sees in her practice. Saying to young Damian, "I don't like your behavior," is certainly better than telling the child he is possessed. But it is not as effective as giving him a specific example of what he is doing wrong so that he knows which behavior to change—"Damian! No squeezing your new baby brother until he turns purple."

Medical students, four-year-olds, writers—we are all alike. When it comes to feedback, we need specifics. In the writing realm, if you are critiquing an early draft, specific feedback might focus on such bigger issues as point of view, structure, or characterization. With a more polished draft, specific feedback might zoom in on scene details or the mechanics of writing. In either extreme of the drafting process, the value of specific feedback is the same. It directs the writer's attention to potential problem areas or opportunities in the text while offering insights into why something is working or not working for you, as a reader. Specific feedback may even go so far as to include "solutions" to the problem or concrete suggestions, which can be useful to the writer as long as you don't present them as mandates. To avoid this, it helps to couch your suggestions in language that reminds the writer whose story it is: "You may want to think about limiting point of view to just one character because this would make me feel more emotionally vested in the story; but of course it's completely your call."

As a feedback provider, you might feel reluctant to offer *any* criticism for fear of hurting the writer's feelings or driving him into a funk. Writers, however, can handle specifics. It's the generalities that bring them to their knees. "Your story didn't work for me." "I don't get it." "This isn't my thing." Those are the kinds of demoralizing conclusions that only serve to leave writers feeling more at a loss than usual. After all, how does a writer revise so that a reader "gets it"? In contrast, writers appreciate detailed responses to their work, which they can use to inform the choices they make during the rewriting process.

In fact, most writers are dependent on feedback providers. After prolonged exposure to their manuscripts, writers often suffer the editorial equivalent of snow blindness. The pages become reduced to a white blur too painful to look at any longer, and without some outside perspective helping to guide them toward the next draft, they can only stagger around blindly, hoping the direction in which they are heading with revision is the right one. With time and distance, writers may regain their vision and return to the terrain of their own manuscripts with more acuity, but it is always much safer and more expedient to have someone by their side, pointing and shouting out when necessary, "Look out for that crevasse!"

Here is an example of how you, as a feedback provider, can turn a generalization into useful, specific feedback:

"Your narrator doesn't work for me." (Now be more specific.)

"Your narrator doesn't work for me because she is mean and I don't like mean people." (Now be even more specific.)

"Your narrator doesn't work for me because she purposely ran over her husband with the car on page 6, but until that point in the story she seemed genuinely to love him. So I don't understand her motivation. I'm not convinced by this sudden personality change."

Now that is valuable feedback, alerting the writer to the fact that she omitted something crucial in the text. Enlightened by the specifics of your response, the writer will react to this feedback not with frustration but with a sense of direction and purpose, knowing that she will spend her next writing session happily developing a scene in which her narrator discovers her husband smooching the attractive new neighbor lady shortly before she turns him into a speed bump.

As this example shows, giving writers specific feedback requires more effort on your part as a critiquer. It is much easier to make generalized assessments—"I was so terribly bored."—than it is to figure out where the piece lost your attention, or why. Some readers fail to offer specific feedback because they are shiftless and their mothers still make their beds. Also, I suspect a few feedback providers secretly enjoy the ego boost that goes along with making autocratic judgments—"I now pronounce this story stultifying!"

Those readers aside, I think most people hesitate to give specific feedback because they lack confidence in their "legitimacy" as a feedback provider, or because they lack the vocabulary of criticism. Certainly, the more experience you have providing feedback, the easier it becomes to analyze and articulate the reasons why you think some aspect of a story needs work. "Here, Mr. Writer, the text disruptively drifts from close third-person to an omniscient point of view. Here, the protagonist's epiphany wasn't manifested in an externalized action. Here, the lyrical prose rhythm is at odds with the scenic tension." Whoa! That's good stuff, very impressive, and if you can critique in those terms, help yourself to burnt coffee in the faculty lounge.

Even if you lack the vocabulary of criticism, however, you can still provide valuable feedback, and the bonus is that your comments won't be cloaked in any literary jargon. For example, you may not know that the most basic form or structure of a story comes down to: conflict, crisis, and resolution. But you do know that you were restless while reading the story until chapter 4, when the upstanding protagonist got that phone call from his old drinking buddy, fresh out of jail. That's specific, useful feedback. You may not know how James Joyce's use of the term *epiphany* applies to literature, but you do know that you felt cheated when the mother in the story didn't seem to be phased one bit after the browbeaten daughter she had depended on for years finally got her own apartment six hundred miles away. That's specific, useful feedback.

Experienced or not in the art of literary analysis, if you simply pay attention to your reactions as you read, you will be able to provide the writer with thoughtful input. What's more, you can take comfort in the fact that your feedback doesn't have to be right—it just has to be sincere. It is up to the writer to weigh your opinions and observations against their own writerly instincts and intentions for the story.

One last point. Most of this chapter focuses on the need for specificity when offering critical feedback. But specificity is also important when it comes to providing positive feedback. "Good job!" "This story is perfect!" "Can I have your autograph?" Of course, secretly, that is *exactly* the kind of feedback all writers think they want to hear when they hand over a manuscript to a critiquer. In reality, though, sweeping affirmations empower the writer only until he begins a new story. Tomorrow, faced with a blank page, with no specific understanding of how he achieved his former success, the writer will be much more inclined to see that last story as a fluke rather than as a cumulative achievement of masterful plotting, vivid characterization, powerful language, and appropriate comma placement.

What's more, sweeping affirmations often backfire. Maybe it is the way humans are hardwired, or maybe it is because a lot of us still believe in the Evil Eye, but most people are loathe to accept compliments of a general nature. You see proof of this all the time. Tell your best friend she looks nice, and she immediately points out the stain on her blouse. Applaud your child on his beautiful painting, and he angrily rips it in half—"Couldn't you see how the bunny's ears don't match!" Say to a writer, "Great story!" and she automatically thinks, *Oh, you're just saying that. This is probably the worst thing I've ever written.*

But if you offer specifics, then people will actually believe you.

"That blue blouse really brings out the color in your eyes."

"I love how the bunny sunning himself on the hill looks so cute."

"Your main character's journey through adolescence reminded me exactly of the restlessness and insecurity of my own childhood."

Positive feedback is more convincing and easier to accept when it is specific. As pediatrician and Harvard professor Beth Rider emphasizes in her workshops, "If you want good behaviors repeated, you need to be descriptive." Whether you are providing positive feedback to medical students, four-year-olds, or writers, you can help them continue to succeed or just feel terrific by letting them know *exactly* what they did right. And for that reason alone the feedback interaction is worth more than the time it takes to ride six floors up in an elevator.

KHALED HOSSEINI:
"EVEN IF THE BOOK IS GOOD, NO ONE IS GOING TO WANT TO PUBLISH IT."

Much of Khaled Hosseini's blockbuster first novel, *The Kite Runner*, is set in his native Afghanistan, a country many Westerners would have had trouble finding on a map before the tragedy of September 11, 2001. The story evolves from the doomed friendship of two Afghani boys—one upper class and one outcast—and spans thirty years of the country's recent history, from the end of the monarchy to the Soviet invasion and the Taliban's reign of terror. Khaled was about halfway through writing the novel when Afghanistan drew the eyes of the world.

Khaled began shopping his novel around to agents in June 2002, less than a year after the United States had bombed Afghanistan in search of Al-Qaeda members. He sent the manuscript to six to eight agents at a time, collecting an early string of rejections. In the midst of this lackluster beginning, he received a particularly crushing letter. One agent reported, "The book is good, but the public doesn't want to hear any more about Afghanistan," Khaled recalls. Afghanistan is passé. That was the agent's implication.

Despite the fact that only two tenuous months had passed since the Afghanistan Grand Council had established an interim government to replace Taliban rule, Khaled was convinced the agent was right. After all, by the summer of 2002 much of the world's focus had shifted to Iraq, with headlines of a possible United States–led invasion bumping any news of Afghanistan to an occasional copy line on the CNN ticker bar. "It felt like a no-win situation," Khaled said. The agent had suggested he should think about writing a book about something else, and he was inclined to agree. "Even if the book is good, no one is going to want to publish it," he recalls thinking. "There was no fix for that. After that feedback, I was in the doldrums."

He stopped sending the book out for a brief period until his wife, Roya, intervened. Khaled had been relying on Roya's editorial advice as he drafted the novel, but now she sounded in with moral support. "She kept pestering me to keep sending the manuscript out to more agents," he laughs. Reluctantly, he followed through, sending the manuscript to six more agents. One of those six was Elaine Koster, who had no doubts about the book's timely appeal. Elaine quickly sold *The Kite Runner* to Riverhead Books, who rushed it into publication in 2003.

In an earlier draft of the book, Khaled's protagonist, Amir, was married to an American woman from Ohio. For some time, Khaled's editor had been suggesting that the wife's character was problematic and that the second half of the book lost much of its cultural flavor. Three weeks before the final manuscript was due, Khaled was still trying to address these issues—tweaking here, tweaking there—when the solution suddenly dawned on him. "I called my editor and said, 'I figured it out! The wife isn't American; she's Afghan!'" Khaled says. His editor agreed; in fact, she had been thinking the same thing, but she had hoped he would come to this realization on his own.

Amazingly, Khaled met his deadline less than a month later. Because he was working full-time as a physician, he would write from 5:00 p.m. until 2:00 in the morning, then fax the pages to Roya, who was pregnant with their second child and staying with her parents for a few weeks. Roya would fax her suggestions back to Khaled, who would revise accordingly then email the new work to his editor. "I felt like I was standing in front of a mountain," Khaled says. "The idea of reinventing, reimagining the whole middle of the book seemed like such a Herculean task. But it's an act of faith. You do what your gut tells you and hope it's right."

And what about that one agent's prediction that a novel about Afghanistan was passé—feedback that almost stopped Khaled from pursuing publication? When *The Kite Runner* first came out, *Publishers Weekly* stated, "It is rare that a book is at once so timely and of such high literary quality." In 2007, the much-loved novel was made into a major motion picture, and the author has followed that powerful debut with two other novels, *A Thousand Splendid Suns* and *And the Mountains Echoed,* in total selling more than 40 million copies worldwide.

Khaled remains grateful about the success of his first novel, which launched the kind of literary career so many aspiring authors can only dream about, but nothing means more to him than the feedback he receives regularly from people wanting to donate money, resources, or goods to Afghans, particularly donations for the children. Khaled tells of one moving note from a couple that had started the process of adopting an Afghan child after reading the book. "I appreciate the reviews and accolades, but this was the real world," Khaled says. "Real people affecting real lives. It goes to show you what a subjective business publishing is."

THE MOMENT OF TRUTH

If you know anything about the University of Iowa Writers' Workshop, you have probably heard stories about the late, great Frank Conroy, who served as the director of the program for eighteen years and loved his job of helping emerging writers. I never went to this prestigious program, and I never met the man, but every article I have read about Conroy makes some mention of his blunt, curmudgeonly approach to teaching creative writing, including his admission to making one student cry and another one faint with his classroom criticism. In a 2004 Associated Press interview, Conroy said with a laugh that it was lucky one of the other students in the fainter's class was a doctor, who realized what was happening and caught her before she hit the ground.

I am not so sure I see the humor in making writers faint, but I do understand that you can't be a good feedback provider if you are not honest about a work's faults or the writer's bad writing habits. ("Personal tics," as Conroy referred to these unintended glitches that show up in the prose.) That is why, in almost every feedback session, there needs to come a Moment of Truth. Criticism, in combination with kindness, is part of your job description. So if you avoid the Moment of Truth, then you and the writer might just as well go roller-skating, or get matching tattoos, or indulge in some other pleasant diversion that isn't intended to enable good writing.

When I was just starting to write this book, I gave one of my first completed chapters to my friend Catherine for feedback. Catherine and I had met when she took one of my fiction-writing workshops a few years earlier, at a time when I was still teaching out of a room in the back of my house. Sometimes, secretly, I use the workshop as a recruiting ground for finding people to enhance my social life, and one evening, when Catherine was the first to show up at a meeting, two things spoke to her potential as a friend: One, she didn't make me feel bad when, to my horror, she spotted a rat running around my kitchen. And two, her youngest daughters were the same ages as my girls. After that meeting, I started pursuing Catherine for lunch dates and play dates; and how could she say no when she still had to face me every Thursday night in our workshop?

After I had given Catherine my chapter for review, three long weeks passed without hearing a response from her. Suffice it to say that three weeks is *way* past the statute of limitations for giving feedback to friends, so I knew that this delay didn't bode well. Instead of being passive and paranoid about the situation, however, I decided to act like an adult. I picked up the phone and called Catherine to arrange another play date, knowing this would corner her into giving me feedback about my chapter.

The next day, Catherine and I were visiting in her living room while our four girls played downstairs in her romper-room basement. The subject of my book happened to come up in the conversation. Actually, I brought it up, partly because of my agenda to force Catherine's feedback, and partly because I talk incessantly about a book when I am working on it, even though I know firsthand that when other writers do this, it gets old, fast. "Did you have a chance yet to read the chapter I gave you a few weeks ago?" I asked casually.

"Another cup of tea?" Catherine answered, and that's when I knew she was stalling for time and that she hadn't liked my chapter at all. I also knew that she knew that I knew that she was stalling for time and hadn't liked my chapter at all, because girlfriends always know when something awkward is unspoken between them. We don't let on directly that anything is amiss, but we do get weirdly polite and start pushing the tea.

Catherine retrieved her copy of my chapter from a nearby desk and took the seat beside me on the couch. Right away, I noticed that the top page didn't bear any line edits or notations. Maybe I had misinterpreted the situation. Maybe Catherine thought my chapter was perfect! Then she asked me again if I wanted a refill of tea, and at that point all hope faded.

Catherine's first few comments about the piece were positive. She pointed out a handful of well-written passages and a few lines she particularly appreciated. Then she hesitated, and we both knew what had to come next—the Moment of Truth. To her credit, Catherine didn't mince words. "I think you need to start over," she said. She went on to explain in the gentlest manner possible how she felt the chapter was disjointed, like a mishmash of thoughts pasted together. She wasn't sure what point I was trying to make. The chapter, in short, didn't have a structure or a message; at least not any that she could discern.

To my credit, I got through the Moment of Truth without doing any of the things I felt like doing—crying, hitting, kicking a bunch of stuffed animals across the room. Given I already had several years of experience as a professional freelance writer and author, I had trained myself to receive criticism with some equanimity, but I was under a tight deadline for this book, and that kind of pressure never helps—or rather it helps enormously, but not in those first few moments when you realize you're clueless and screwed, and you just want to be *done*.

One part of my brain started thrashing my ego—*Bad writer! Idiot! You'll never be able to write a book about feedback!* Yet (here's where that training and equanimity started to kick in) even while I was silently catastrophizing, another part of my brain was registering Catherine's insights. Just as every good feedback provider has a responsibility to arrive at the Moment of Truth, every feedback receiver, too, has a responsibility to keep it together enough to face the Truth, and to use it to become a stronger writer.

I know it was hard for Catherine as a feedback provider, and especially as a friend, to speak honestly about my chapter. The best feedback providers are well aware of the emotional impact of their words. Sometimes, no matter how kindly you package your criticism, you can never eliminate the wince factor completely.

I spoke about this issue with a workshop instructor and author in Chicago named Enid Powell, who had been teaching adult writing students for over twenty years. In her former life as a writer for a soap opera, Enid had experienced plenty of toxic feedback in a working environment where favored writers received gold stars on their scripts while others were reduced to a "puddle of shame." Enid wanted none of that toxicity in her own workshops. "If I find myself frustrated or upset when I'm giving feedback, I stop," she said, "because if I don't critique with love, they won't understand what I'm trying to say."

Enid came upon this sudden insight in the middle of editing a manuscript, and it was a shock. "I had to stop and do something else, to remind myself of my affection for the writer and for her work in the past," she explained. "This time-out seemed to give my brain time to think of solutions to the problem, instead of the blind *No, No, No* that comes when frustration makes me blank out."

The need to curb any impatience with the writer also applies during story discussions, Enid shared. "Recently, I found myself about to interrupt three times during the lengthy reading of a manuscript, and not with a kindly, 'Excuse me, I think we've heard enough.' Thank God I stopped myself," she added. "It would have been disastrous. I would have lost the trust this person places in me to even have the courage to tackle a difficult topic. By staying silent, I gained time to remind myself of the vulnerability of all my writers; then I could think more clearly about what was salvageable in her work, so that the discussion ended on a positive note." Enid continued, "My goal is to keep people writing, and to prove to them that when they say, 'Nobody will be interested in this,' they're wrong."

Enid also told me about the time she was critiquing a novel and realized that the writer needed to switch the point of view from third person to first person for a variety of convincing reasons. (One being that, with three female protagonists, the third-person perspective created a confusion of "she's".) Enid felt so bad, yet certain, about the need for this significant change that she offered to retype the writer's entire manuscript for her.

For all of you feedback providers who are softies like Enid, here is a comforting thought. The Moment of Truth is just that—a moment, relatively speaking. Once you put forth your constructive criticism, you can then move on to happier discussion topics, like the remarkable power of revision and where the writer might go from here.

After Catherine told me I needed to start over with my chapter, she began asking me questions, the first one being, "What exactly are you trying to communicate in this piece?" Our subsequent conversation not only distracted me from my misery, it also enabled me to clarify my thinking and regroup. Eventually I understood why the chapter failed. One reason was because the introduction was a leftover from an earlier draft in which I had focused the chapter differently. I had been too lazy and enamored with the writing to let it go, so I had revised the lede to death, hoping to save it and avoid extra work. With the realization that I needed to abandon the opening entirely, the rewriting process had already begun, and the wince factor had already started to diminish.

Thanks to the Moment of Truth, I saw that my point—and I did have one—could rise from the ashes and be reborn as a new chapter, but only if I got a fresh start, didn't cut corners, and scheduled a few more play dates.

COMMON HUMAN DECENCY

For decades, Houghton Mifflin has published its annual edition of *The Best American Short Stories,* an anthology of twenty or so stories culled from thousands that were published in magazines and literary publications in the United States and Canada the previous year. The series editor also chooses an additional hundred short stories of distinction and lists them by title and author in the back of the book.

Several years ago, my friend (I'll call her Lisa here) discovered that a short story of hers was listed among the honored one hundred in the back pages. She learned this happy news when she was skimming through the anthology in a bookstore, debating whether she could afford to shell out the $16.95 to buy her own copy. Suddenly, amid the usual autonyms—Alice Munro, Lorrie Moore, John Updike—she spied her own name and story title bouncing off the page like a bright dot from one of those inadvisable laser pointers. This came as quite a surprise. Until then, Lisa hadn't even been aware that her story, originally published in a small literary journal, was in the running for this lofty collection. Given the circumstances, she decided to spring for the book.

I still find it hard to believe that this—this happenstance—is how my friend learned that a story of hers had been chosen as one of America's most distinguished for that year. Every time I think about it, I just can't get past the "what ifs." What if Lisa hadn't bothered to browse through the back of the book? What if she had *never* learned about this honor? What if she had spent her whole life assuming that her name and the name of Alice Munro had never graced the same list of distinguished authors. And what if this assumption had eventually led her to stop writing and degenerate into someone sad and pathetic, say an HGTV addict, reeking of handcrafted pomander balls, surrounded by wicker trash baskets converted into kitschy side tables and surviving on stale-but-still-edible picture frames? This didn't happen to my friend Lisa, but I'm sure it has happened to some writer, somewhere, who didn't know her work was appreciated.

Which begs the question: Why *didn't* the editor at Houghton Mifflin simply send an email to tell Lisa the good news? "Dear Writer, Congratulations! We loved your story and selected it as one of this year's most distinguished. Signed, the Editor." Even a text with the usual acronyms would have sufficed. "JSYK, YTB. GL!" (Translation: Just so you know, you're the best. Good luck!) Dashing off a quick note is such a simple gesture, but think of how much an acknowledgment of this nature might mean to a writer. So why-oh-why didn't the editor take the time to let those shortlisted authors know they'd been shortlisted?

I can tell you why, though if you have had any experience querying editors or sending submissions out to magazines or publishing houses, you probably know the answer. Editors have no common human decency. This is not a statement on their character. (Having once been an editor of a regional magazine, I can attest to the fact that at least some editors are actually quite nice in real life.) No, a lack of common human decency is simply a requirement of the job, as delineated in *The Professional Editor's Handbook,* Rule No. 7,849: "Editors must refrain from exhibiting any form of compassion, enthusiasm, interest, or basic manners toward writers at large."

The reason for this rule is perfectly obvious. Editors who exhibit even the slightest sign of common human decency run the risk of desperate, aspiring authors (of which there are legions) inundating them with queries about their latest scintillating story ideas, their passion for the written word, and their unpaid Visa bills, all under the misguided notion that one innocent, supportive gesture constituted an "in." No busy editor—routinely beleaguered by time, budget, and page constraints—can afford to take this risk. Hence Rule No. 7,849. And hence the necessity for the biggest indecency of them all: the form rejection letter, used even for cases where the submission may be excellent, but the fit isn't. ("Doesn't meet our needs.")

Here, gentle reader, I am going to presume that you are not a professional editor at a magazine or publishing house. As such, you are not required to curb your enthusiasm around writers at large, and your behavior should conform to an entirely different set of rules, with Rule No. 1 being: If you like someone's work, tell them! Otherwise, your silence becomes a form of toxic feedback, forcing the writer to make assumptions about how you feel about her writing. And allowing writers to assume anything is never a good idea because they will always assume the worst.

You would think that a feedback provider who actually enjoyed a writer's efforts would jump at the opportunity to tell her so. After all, how often is it that we get to spread a little good news for a change? Yet, remarkably, readers frequently fail to show enthusiasm, or even respond, to writers whose work they enjoyed. Making this silent treatment all the more peculiar is that oftentimes these very same readers had invited, sometimes even nagged, the writer to share her work with them. Once the manuscript is received, however, some trait in these readers (perhaps cluelessness, laziness, or a tad bit of jealousy) prevents them from extending their congratulations on a job well done.

Equally perplexing is when a reader / feedback provider volunteers only a stingy or cryptic response to a submission, which sometimes can be worse for the writer than no response at all. Here is one example of this (which happened to me), but I have heard dozens of similar tales. Recently, I asked a writer friend to look over a finished essay before I submitted it to a publisher. In the cover note, I also asked him to verify the spelling of his name because he was referenced in the piece. A few days later, I received his feedback: "My name is spelled correctly." For days, I fumed about this pathetic excuse for a response. No *halloo!* No *Nice of you to check in.* No, *Great job, you amazing creature!* Finally, unable to let it go, I emailed this person back. "Just curious . . ." I wrote. "What did you think about the essay?" His response: "I thought it was EXCELLENT!" All caps.

So why didn't he say so in the first place?

Writers work hard, often with little or no pay. They also spend way too much time thinking and inferring. For these reasons and many more, writers need and deserve some honest gushing over their successes. Yes, once a story or a book is accepted, editors are often effusive in their praise, but during the writer's long and arduous journey toward publication (if that is the writer's goal), external validation, heartfelt compliments, or even just a smiley-face emoticon can be ridiculously hard to come by. This is not right. Not right at all. Praise nourishes the ego, and writers—to be able to continue doing what they do—need all the ego they can get.

So here is an entreaty to readers and feedback providers everywhere, including workshop participants, writing instructors, friends, spouses, colleagues, parents, and anyone else who doesn't work as a professional editor at a magazine or a publishing house: Show a little common human decency.

When you read someone's work and like it, make a point to say so. Don't make the writer ask twice. Don't hold back. Don't worry about looking like a crazed fan. Chase the writer down an alley if you have to, waving her manuscript over your head and shouting at her retreating form, "I loved your story! I loved your story!" At the very least, drop her a form affirmation email: Dear Writer, Your work really met my needs!!! Signed, [your name here].

Small Addendum

Gentle reader, on the off chance that you actually do work as an editor at a magazine or publishing house, I would like to say for the record that when I made that statement about editors having no common human decency, I meant that in a *good* way. And because you are a professional editor who has clearly taken a personal interest in my work—Why else would you be reading this book?—I am sure you wouldn't mind sending me your contact information so that I can tell you all about my latest scintillating book idea, and my passion for the written word, and my unpaid Visa bills. Better yet, I am free for lunch tomorrow and every day in the foreseeable future. Just let me know what works best for you!

DON (D. B.) JOHNSON:
"MY BEST ADVICE IS TO MARRY WELL."

I was going to meet Don (D. B.) Johnson at an upscale coffee bar to talk about his award-winning picture-book series that conceptualizes Henry David Thoreau in the form of a cubist-style bear. But the coffee bar wasn't open when we arrived, so we moved our meeting outside to a picnic table under a tree. This turned out to be a much more fitting setting for a conversation with a writer and illustrator who grew up in rural New Hampshire, loves nature, and has spent much of his adult life trying to reconcile the desire to be an artist with the reality of needing to earn a living. "If you live in the country with three kids, you do a lot of justifying," Don smiled.

For more than twenty years, Don worked as a freelance illustrator, first doing editorial cartoons for newspapers around the country and then taking more lucrative, corporate assignments. About once a year he picked up his copy of *Walden* and reread it, inspired by Thoreau's defense of living the creative life. In one passage, Thoreau recounted the story of how a friend suggested he travel to Fitchburg by train, to which Thoreau countered that it would be faster to walk the thirty miles than to earn the ninety cents to pay for the ticket. In 1991 Don noted this passage in his "idea file," thinking it might make a good story.

Seven years later, having just returned from a trip to Russia to visit his son, Don found himself back in his studio without any work. Rummaging through his idea file, he saw the reference he had made to Thoreau. "It was serendipity," Don recalled. His trip to Russia had reminded him of his own childhood, seeing clothes on the line and experiencing life without so many modern conveniences. While there, he had even taken a train ride to the Russian countryside. "Everything came together," Don said, and he knew it was time to act on his idea. He would create a picture book—a series of picture books, actually—embodying Thoreau's beliefs, starting with a story centered around Thoreau's passage on why it was faster to walk to Fitchburg.

Because Don thought of himself as an illustrator, not a writer, he asked his wife, Linda, to write the text that would accompany his illustrations. She declined, saying Thoreau was his passion and that he should write the story. "She was right," Don ceded, and two months later he had finished the manuscript and a sample illustration. Two weeks after he sent the work off to Houghton Mifflin, they called with an offer. Published in 2000, *Henry Hikes to Fitchburg* became a *New York Times* best seller and won the Ezra Jack Keats New Writer Award and *Publishers Weekly* Best Book of the Year. Since then, Don has made a distinct mark in the world of children's literature, adding more Thoreau-inspired picture books as well as stories that introduce young readers to the foundational ideas of George Orwell, M. C. Escher, and René Magritte. He also created a series of animated e-books for kids, and most recently he launched his Lost Woods comic, also inspired by his love of all things Thoreau.

For the majority of his career, Don found his most useful feedback close to home, referring to the fact that his wife, Linda Michelin, was a writer who often served as his editor. The couple had been married forty-seven years when Linda passed away in 2018. "My best advice is to marry well," he offered. "I think all my ideas are good, but they probably aren't. Having a spouse or friend who can evaluate your work gives you clarity of reason. It's impossible to judge your own writing."

Don also values the feedback he receives from his young readers, whom he describes as "the best audience ever because they are so open. It doesn't matter if they haven't heard of Thoreau, or pick up on the social issues in the books, as long as they like the story." After a reading in Boston of *Henry Hikes to Fitchburg* (which makes the point that you don't need money to get somewhere; you can just put on your boots and go), one little girl in the audience recommended he write another book—Henry Goes Shopping. "She thought I should do a story about Henry going to the mall," Don laughed. "It just goes to show, you can't get to kids soon enough."

But if young readers don't always recognize Thoreau's influence in Don's books, most of their parents do. Feedback from adults about the series and its meditations on materialism, nature, and individualism has been overwhelmingly positive, not surprising given the fact that a *Newsweek* poll listed Thoreau among the top ten most respected American figures.

Don (D. B.) Johnson

For some parents, however, Henry the bear's affinity with his independent-thinking namesake makes him suspect as a character in a children's book. At one public appearance a mother said to Don, "I hope you're not planning to do any Henry books about civil disobedience," a reference to Thoreau's 1849 essay on the right and obligation to follow your conscience, even if it means breaking the law. At the time, Don hadn't been planning to do a story around this issue, but the woman's comment inspired his next book, *Henry Climbs a Mountain*. In that story, Henry is sent to jail for refusing to pay a poll tax as a matter of principle. While in prison, he draws a picture on his cell wall of a mountain, which he then escapes into and climbs, demonstrating that you can lock up a person's body, but not his mind. "I owe that mother a lot," Don said.

From the inception of Henry the bear, Don had planned to write just three books in the series. He had a change of heart, however, after several parents commented on Henry's friend in the first book, who works all day at odd jobs in order to earn his train fare to Fitchburg. "Some of the parents thought I was trying to undermine the idea of work," Don explained, "when what I was trying to do was to expand readers' ideas about what work could be." To address this issue, Don decided to write a fourth book, *Henry Works*, which shows that writing, too, is a form of labor, even if its value isn't always measured by income.

"As a writer, you are taking a chance on yourself whenever you write a proposal or take months or years to write something," Don pointed out. "Writers take risks, and part of that risk is being seen as that lame person who doesn't have a job." Like Thoreau and his eponymous bear, Don believes that people should spend less time working to earn money and more time doing the things that interest them. He knows from personal experience that it isn't always easy to put that philosophy into practice. "I respect people," he added, "who buck the system in that way."

EDITORIAL BIASES

I can't stand it when pets die in stories. In fact, I like to think that if I had been Steinbeck's editor when he wrote *The Red Pony,* I could have saved generations of kids a lot of wasted heartache. This is one of my editorial biases, and so whenever I am critiquing a story in which a pet is killed or even injured, I try my hardest to make the writer change it. All my students and clients know this about me. One of them, a family doctor who has produced a terrific and growing collection of short fiction, once tried to get away with having his main character throw a cat against the wall. The protagonist was drunk, and his behavior was in keeping with his character. The scene fed into the climax of the story beautifully. As if I cared.

"Change it," I demanded.

Every feedback provider comes with editorial biases. These are predispositions or conditioned responses we have picked up along the way that can adversely affect the quality of our feedback. For instance, maybe you are biased against a certain genre of fiction or toward a particular poetic paradigm. Or maybe you hate freckle-faced characters or love *New Yorker*–type stories (or at least you *say* you love *New Yorker*–type stories). Unlike your editorial instincts, which shape your feedback according to what you believe is best for the work, your editorial biases shape your feedback in a way that often says more about *you* than about the writing.

As feedback providers, it is important we set aside our editorial biases in order to provide impartial feedback. Of course, there really is no such thing as impartial feedback (after all, we are humans, not robots), but the notion—similar to the concept of absolute zero—still provides a useful baseline, however theoretical. For example, if I weren't so biased against animal cruelty in fiction, what would I have said to the workshop participant who had his protagonist throw the cat against the wall? The answer to that question moves me closer to impartial feedback by several degrees. It also showcases the gap that can exist between your editorial instincts and your editorial biases, and how the latter can easily compromise the former.

So how do you learn to recognize your editorial biases in order to set them aside when critiquing a work? The first place to look is genetics. Some people are born liking science fiction while other people's DNA makes it impossible for them to understand why anyone would attend a Star Trek convention, even to people-watch. To figure out your genetic editorial biases, just picture the kinds of books you buy when no one is looking. Now picture the kinds of books you wouldn't be caught dead buying unless required to for a class or a book group. There you go. These are your genetic editorial biases, all lined up for you on your mental bookshelf.

If you were just reading for pleasure, these biases wouldn't matter so much because the only person you need to please is yourself (though I would strongly advise branching out once in a while). As a feedback provider, however, your purpose is to serve the writer, which means your tastes are not only irrelevant, but they could get in the way if they predispose you to liking or hating a piece before you have even read it.

Your first inclination might be to disqualify yourself from critiquing a piece written in a genre or style you don't normally read. No. That is not an option in a workshop, where your commitment is to help every writer in the group, not just the ones who write to your sensibilities. So when you do sit down to critique something in good faith, you must try your hardest not to railroad the writer. Otherwise, if you are into neosurrealism poetry, for example, you may find yourself challenging the poet-submitter to break the boundaries of syntax and shoot for a little less intellectual authority and a lot more edge, despite the fact that what he has presented for critique is a Petrarchan sonnet. Similarly, if your taste in novels runs to happy endings, you may push the writer to have the protagonist get the girl or the boy in the end, despite the writer's clear intent of a bitter resolution, where the hero fails to secure what he wants or needs. In situations like these, it is important to remind yourself, *This isn't my work. This isn't about me. It's about helping the writer achieve his goals for the story in the most effective way possible.*

The fact is, even if you are reviewing a work that falls outside the realm of your usual reading habits, you can still provide the writer with useful information. After all, much of the criteria of good writing applies across the board. Did the work create an emotional response? Is it memorable? Are the characters' actions credible? Is the fictional universe well established? Do any scenes feel underdeveloped? Is the language clear or confusing? Plus, here is a bonus. By having to thoughtfully critique a work in a genre or style you don't normally read, you are likely to discover its unique qualities and strengths, and maybe even expand your own reading tastes.

In addition to our genetic editorial biases, we also acquire biases from external sources. And the weird thing about a lot of these acquired biases is that they often have less to do with how we actually feel about a piece of writing and more to do with how we *think* we should feel about the work.

Say you go to a writing program that proselytizes minimalist fiction, or "K-Mart Realism," as novelist Thomas Wolfe negatively referred to the proliferation of Raymond Carveresque stories, with spare prose and a focus on small (but meaningful) moments in the main character's limited life. Before you know it, you may be introjecting the program's editorial biases into your own feedback—discouraging stylistic variation or alternative forms of narrative—without even being aware that you are doing this. If everyone else in the class follows suit, you can see why some MFA programs are accused of promulgating homogeneous writing and are branded as "cookie cutter." A similar phenomenon can happen in critique groups, especially if one of the members has Rasputin-like powers that sway everybody else's feedback and writing style.

The media and publishing industry also serve to shape our editorial biases, influencing our feedback by telling us what is or isn't on trend. (I recently listened to a podcast where, I swear, the publisher used the word "on trend" eight million times.) In addition, social or cultural expectations affect feedback. My friend Bindi is a short-story writer who immigrated to America with her Sikh parents when she was five years old. Bindi can't write about an Indian woman protagonist without at least one critiquer suggesting she focus the story on an arranged marriage, or the issue of being caught between two cultures. "It's as if every Indian story has to contain those particular thematic landmarks in order to be legitimate," she says. Bringing these kinds of expectations to your feedback sends the wrong messages to the writer: "Stick to the standards." "Don't veer from popular themes." "Don't innovate."

In addition, biases can creep into our feedback because of how we feel about a writer personally. There is no denying that when we sit down to critique a manuscript, we all have a tendency to go easier on someone we like and be more dismissive of someone who gets on our nerves. Some classes attempt to sidestep the issue of personal biases by making the writers anonymous, but to me this tactic feels like a charade. When I was giving feedback in a class that did this, I couldn't concentrate on the story discussion because I was so obsessed with trying to figure out who wrote it. And when my own story was on the table, the only thing I could think about was not giving myself away. *Don't look nervous! Don't jot down any notes! Should I make comments to throw people off, or say nothing?* Given all these distractions, it seems to me the better solution to overcoming personal biases is simply to rise above them. React to the work, not the writer. Let's all critique like grown-ups.

For better or worse, we would not be who we are if it weren't for how nature and nurture have shaped our tastes, proclivities, and idiosyncrasies, literary and otherwise. Regardless, having editorial biases doesn't mean you can't be an excellent feedback provider on all kinds of writing by all kinds of writers. I have seen proof of this over and over—how a group member who abhorred horror novels learned to critique one skillfully and without judgment; how a critiquer who only read action adventure came to appreciate the equally intense firepower of women's fiction (why does that term—women's fiction—always sound a bit disparaging?); and how two group members who disliked each other in real life still managed to provide one another with supportive and thoughtful critiques.

As for me, I am getting better at overcoming my own editorial biases, though I still have a lot of room for improvement. I see a lot of fancy-pants, up-front description, and my knee-jerk reaction is to slash it out, without even considering that some readers enjoy fancy-pants description. I read certain kinds of foreshadowing ("Young Sarah didn't know it at the time, but this was to be the last day of her childhood innocence"), and the manuscript is flying out of my hands before I even stop to consider whether this is my issue or the writer's. I see a confusion of characters, and my first recommendation is to simplify—"Give the couple two children instead of four"; "Send the visiting relatives back to their own flea-infested apartment." But is my bias toward simplicity in keeping with the writer's intent, or my own need for peace and quiet?

As a feedback provider, my goal is not only to give the writer my honest response to her work but also to understand where that response is coming from, just in case it is coming from some inexorable, narrow-minded windbag inside of me who can't understand all this fuss over gluten. All this to say, if I recognize any editorial biases creeping into my feedback, I need to revise my comments accordingly, or at least present my feedback with a warning—"Heads up, writer! I despise blatant foreshadowing with the white-hot intensity of a thousand suns, so you might want to think twice before following my advice to cut it all out." That said, even if you are uncertain whether your feedback is biased or not, I do think it is better to speak up than remain silent. Otherwise, you are not giving the writer the benefit of the doubt that he can determine for himself whether to ignore or act on your feedback. My personal credo is simply to do my best to give feedback that serves the story and not just my own tastes . . . with one glaring exception.

Remember that family doctor in my workshop who had his protagonist throw the cat against the wall? Well, he refused to follow my demand to change this. In the story the cat dies of a broken neck. (It pains me to write about it even now.) But the good news is, I still see this writer on a regular basis, and I am still pushing hard for a miracle cure for the cat. Because, bias or not, pets should *never* be killed or even injured in stories.

GET THAT LOOK OFF YOUR FACE

When I was growing up, my parents had no tolerance for whining or self-absorption, which I think was the main reason I felt put out much of the time. How could I appreciate an otherwise happy childhood when the world did not always revolve around me? As a result, I spent much of my youth moping and preoccupied with my own sorry circumstances, though I knew better than to voice aloud my bad attitude. My mother wasn't fooled by my stoic silence. "Get that look off your face," she would always be telling me.

Fast-forward to a few months ago. I received a phone call from a retired surgeon in his early seventies, who invited me to lunch at a swanky, historical inn. He had just finished writing a memoir, and his wife had heard about me when the local paper did a piece on my writer's center. This gentleman wanted my advice about getting published, a subject I am asked about on a regular basis. I do know the drill—writers have three main options: find an agent willing to submit your work to a traditional publisher that, upon acceptance, pays you for the right to publish your book; work with a hybrid publisher that will charge you for their assistance in publishing your book, but the back-end benefit is the potential of higher royalties; or go the self-publishing route, where you act as your own publisher by blogging or selling your work through Amazon, for example (though I hesitate to even write the word *Amazon* given its reputation for killing bookstores).

So yes, I do have insights about the various paths to publication, but the question makes me uneasy because, inside, I still feeling like a desperate wannabe. My advice on how to get published? Google how to get published, and then prepare to feel like Joan Crawford's adopted daughter in *Mommy Dearest* every time you check your inbox—"No wire hangers! No wire hangers ever!"

The gentleman and I met at the swanky, historical inn, wonderfully genteel with its sun-faded, floral wallpaper, white tablecloths laden with delicate china, and a preponderance of diners of a certain age sporting tweed jackets and pocketbooks with clasps. My host, whose broad surgeon hands still looked capable of massaging a human heart back to life, invited me to start the meal with a glass of wine. Who was I to argue? Here was an alternate universe, far removed from my own reality at home all day, writing in my holey jeans, lunching on some microwaved leftovers, just me and my plus-sized cat stretched out on whatever manuscript pages I was trying to edit at the moment. Now, looking at the elegantly etched faces surrounding me in this lovely dining room, it occurred to me that I needed to get out more, or at least make more money so I could save up for a facelift.

Over crab cakes, the gentleman asked me about my writing and my life. As usual when I am talking about myself, the time passed quickly and pleasantly. Late in the meal, however, the conversation turned to his memoir, which he told me he had been urged to write by his wife and several of his friends. I have noticed that memoirists do this a lot; they bring up the fact that someone else was behind their decision to write their personal story, as if they need second-party validation to justify a book about their lives.

"I think everyone should write a memoir," I reassured him sincerely. "Lots of them in fact." That last remark might have been the wine talking, but I really do believe that every person has memories worth chronicling and sharing. Memoirs only disappoint because of how they are rendered, not because the writer isn't a worthy subject. "No, I'm sorry, your life doesn't qualify for a memoir. Now, if you had been a YouTube influencer or a superhero . . . Next!"

I asked the gentleman if he had started looking for an agent, remembering that the purpose of this lunch was to talk about publishing.

"I've done a bit of research," he said, dismissing his efforts with a shrug.

"The ideal agent is a compassionate barracuda," I announced, borrowing this phrase from one of my successful novelist friends. I wasn't sure this observation qualified as useful advice, but I have always liked saying it and pretending it was my own.

"Actually, I'm not really interested in agents or publishers at the moment," the gentleman confessed, after the waitress had removed our empty plates and refilled our coffee. "I've been toiling alone on this memoir for two years now, and what I really want is an outside perspective. I was wondering," he paused to take a sip of his decaf, and I thought I noted a slight tremor in his surgeon hands, "if you might possibly consider reading the book and offering me some feedback?"

Oh my. This was a different situation entirely, one that required more than committing myself to a leisurely, free lunch. The gentleman hastened to add that he would pay me for my services, but by this time I was feeling more than a little cornered and guilty about having hogged most of the conversation. Plus, I had made a point of ordering dessert because I wasn't the one picking up the tab. So I told him I would read his memoir, and that lunch was payment enough, though that last part was definitely the wine talking.

Three weeks later, I was driving to the gentleman's house at 7:45 a.m. with a bad attitude, a travel mug of espresso, and my copy of his 186-page manuscript that I had earmarked with suggestions and edits. I had scheduled the feedback session as early as possible because I wanted to keep the rest of the workday free. I had my own writing to do, which wasn't going well, deadlines were looming, and I felt puffy. At stoplights, I drummed my fingers on the steering wheel and glared at the manuscript on the passenger seat, reminding me of all the hours I had lost in the past few weeks reviewing somebody else's work when what I really needed was to somehow salvage my own.

When the gentleman opened his front door, I was greeted by the smell of freshly baked cranberry muffins. He offered me one and apologized for Snowball, the cat, who was circling my legs and fuzzing up my black tights. I noticed that the writer had set out on the breakfast table a clean copy of his memoir with two sharpened pencils beside it. From a room in the back of the apartment, his wife appeared. "Be merciful," she said by way of greeting, then she quickly retreated, followed by Snowball, either to escape or to give us some privacy.

Thank goodness for the little things that jar us out of our own snits. Maybe it was the travel mug of espresso I had downed on the ride over, or maybe it was the wife's "be merciful" before she backed out of the room, but I think it was seeing those two sharpened pencils poised for note-taking on whatever I had to say that made me suddenly aware that I needed an attitude adjustment. Here I was, standing in a writer's kitchen, exuding negativity and impatience. The fact that I wasn't complaining or whining aloud meant nothing. I had, as my mother used to point out, that look on my face, plain enough for even Snowball to realize he had better leave me the hell alone.

You cannot be a good feedback provider if you have a bad attitude. Attitude is huge in affecting outcomes; this is true in any realm of life, from weathering disease to landing that promotion. As a feedback provider, attitude affects the way you approach a critique; are you focused on the writer's needs or your own? Attitude affects the way you frame your comments; is your language encouraging or disdainful? Attitude also affects how the writer reacts to your input; will he be receptive to your suggestions and gain confidence, or will he feel smote from the black energy emoting from your ears and never want to share his work again?

For me, the crazy thing is that I love giving writers feedback, but that still doesn't stop me from falling into snits. This has nothing to do with the quality of a manuscript and everything to do with my recurring, childish tendency to feel put out when the world does not revolve around me. When the gentleman had delivered the draft of his memoir to me, I had felt the heft of those 186 pages, and all I could think about was how much work I had ahead of me. I didn't have time for this. Why had I been stupid enough to refuse payment? What the heck did this newly retired surgeon want from me? I bet he had never operated on anyone for free!

Later, standing in the writer's kitchen, confronted by those two sharpened pencils, I was reminded in the nick of time that the real effort was on the gentleman's part. Two years of work had gone into drafting this memoir. Not just work, but heart. This situation wasn't about me. It was all about the writer—his issues, his needs. I had no right to undermine his effort by projecting negativity. I also wasn't doing myself any favors. By focusing so narrowly on my own dark thoughts, I was bound to miss out on the real enjoyment that comes from helping someone improve their work.

And so, I got that look off my face. I consciously shook off my bad attitude and replaced it with a positive one. I did this not by changing my personality (*as if*), but by shifting my focus to the writer. Giving feedback is an opportunity to relate to another person in a truly meaningful way; an opportunity that will be squandered if we do not make a point to engage wholeheartedly in the process. We owe it to the writer to be upbeat, even if that means manufacturing our enthusiasm at first. But here is the nice thing: by simply making the effort, real positivism usually follows.

For two hours, the gentleman and I bent our heads together over manuscript pages sprinkled with cranberry-muffin crumbs. Here it is important to note that while I changed my attitude, I did not change the main message of my feedback. The memoir needed work. The writer had captured key events in his life vibrantly through scenes, yet the scenes needed to be more thematically connected, shaped into a central narrative with an endpoint. The difference, however, was that now my message had a much better context. My attitude made it clear—I valued this gentleman's writing. I was on his side. And I knew, with additional effort and three or seven more drafts, he *would* shape his memoir into a very fine book. Of that, I was truly positive.

TED KOOSER:
"WE ALL SERVE COMMUNITIES."

The same week Ted Kooser found out he had been appointed to serve a second term as America's poet laureate, he also received the 2005 Pulitzer Prize for Poetry for his book *Delights and Shadows*. Pretty extraordinary events for a man whose verse focuses on the ordinary—spring plowing, walking to work, laundry, a grandfather's cap. The first US laureate from the Plains States, the Nebraska writer has published fifteen collections of poetry that have earned him numerous prizes and honors over the years, including two National Endowment for the Arts fellowships and the Pushcart Prize. In addition, Ted has published nonfiction works and, most recently, has turned his attention to writing for children. He is also the Presidential Professor Emeritus at the University of Nebraska, where he taught the writing of poetry.

Ted has been described as sharing the perspective of the "average American," yet it is his ability to illuminate in a flash the beauty and significance of everyday moments that sets him apart. His poems are short; his style accessible. "I never want to be thought of as pandering to a broad audience," he once told an interviewer, "but you can tweak a poem just slightly and broaden the audience very much. If you have a literary allusion, you limit the audience. Every choice requires a cost-benefit analysis." Spoken like a true insurance executive, which was his day job for thirty-five years before retiring in 1999.

In his poem "Selecting a Reader," Ted describes a woman in a dirty raincoat thumbing through one of his poetry collections then returning it to the shelf. "For that kind of money, I can get my raincoat cleaned," the woman says in the poem. "And she will," Ted concludes in the last line. "Writers need to remember that readers have priorities," he says. "Sometimes it's a lot more important to have a clean raincoat than a new book."

He also understands readers' impatience with poetry that is hard to understand. When Ted worked at the insurance company he would sometimes run poems-in-progress by his secretary to test them for clarity. In the end, a verse that appears straightforward may have taken forty or fifty drafts, demonstrating the truth that the art is to hide the art. As a poet and a promoter of poetry, it is Ted's blend of accessibility and artistry that has helped academics and mainstream readers find—and appreciate—common ground.

How do you use feedback when you write?

I have several writer friends with whom I correspond about my poetry. In exchange, I look at their poems on request. When I have a fairly satisfactory draft of a poem, I send it to one or more of these people, either by email or regular post, and they generously offer comments. They might point to an awkward usage, or a clumsy grammatical construction, or even a misspelled word. It is understood that they wouldn't criticize the general thrust of the poem, only the mechanics.

When you teach and do workshops, how do you use feedback to help students?

I treat my students pretty much the same way that I described my friends treating me. I go for specifics: problems of usage, clumsiness, and so forth.

How would you recommend writers use the feedback process?

It's good to find a reader for your work who will be specific with his or her comments. It doesn't help to have somebody say, "I like this," or, "This is interesting." You need to have specific suggestions, like, "There's an apostrophe in line five that confuses me."

What's the biggest danger when it comes to applying feedback to poetry?

One must be careful not to make use of the suggestions of others unless they have made a really persuasive argument. You don't want them writing your poem, and sometimes you have to refuse to let go of your own way of writing. There have been times when I've tried to follow suggestions and wound up ruining the poem.

Ted Kooser

Do you have a "best" feedback story?

When I was a very young writer, Robert Bly read a poem of mine and said, simply, "You're making it up." He meant that I was using my imagination to furnish the poem, and he wanted me to actually observe the subject, carefully, and write from the real experience. I found that very helpful. I made a number of changes in the poem before it was published, but it has been too long ago for me to remember them precisely. But it was Robert's helpful comment that set me on the right track for a successful revision.

As Poet Laureate, how did you encourage people to read more poetry?

I think the best sell was to show them poems that I think they would be able to relate to. That was really the purpose of my newspaper column,* to provide examples of poems that can move people but still be relatively easy to understand. Teaching by example is the preferred method here.

When you give readings, what is the general tenor of the feedback?

I have been deeply gratified by the responses I've had. Many people have come up to me after a reading and told me that they appreciated it, that I seemed to be writing for them or that I was taking their lives into consideration.

Any final thoughts about feedback?

We all serve communities, and because of this it is important to think about the community into which you direct your writing. You should choose your outside readers from the community you wish to reach with your work. For example, if your intended audience is a broad segment of the population who don't have PhDs in English, you should choose an outside reader from that community.

---

* Ted launched the newspaper column "American Life in Poetry," which he edited for fifteen years, producing more than eight hundred columns. The column is now curated and edited by Kwame Dawes and can be viewed online as well as in select papers.

FOUR BREATHS IN.
FOUR BREATHS OUT.

When the story on the table is about a personal trauma, and the feedback interaction goes awry, it can feel like the worst kind of awry.

Imagine, for example, a writer who has submitted scenes from her memoir about the accidental death of her one-year-old daughter. She has managed to relive this terrible experience on the page and bring her manuscript to her critique group. One gentleman tries to comfort her by talking about God's will. Another member of the group puts on her untrained-therapist hat and encourages the writer to talk about her feelings. Another effuses empathy, to such a degree that the mother of the lost child feels obliged to comfort her. Meanwhile, the rest of the participants remain silent because who are they to pick on the writer's stilted dialogue when this bereaved woman has lost a child. It just doesn't seem right.

It isn't right, that children die.

Let's take a few moments. Maybe sit in stillness, or silent prayer, or reflection. Four breaths in, four breaths out.

Now consider this mother who lost her daughter, and the courage it took to not only relive such a horror on the paper, but to then share her manuscript for critique. That double-display of courage is precisely why you owe it to her to manage your own feelings and dignify her efforts. Given you are together in a critique group, or have some kind of writing relationship, you can assume she shared her pages for a specific purpose—to hear thoughtful feedback that will help her turn her personal tragedy into meaningful prose for people other than herself.

When true stories about difficult subject matter are presented in my classes (an understandably frequent experience, given writing about personal trauma is one of the most effective ways to process, draw meaning from, or even survive the pain), I need those few moments of stillness. In that liminal space I am suspended between my own emotional reaction to the subject matter . . . and what must come next, which is my reaction not to the tragedy, but to the text. Yes, a child died. But is the story well framed? Are there point-of-view issues? Are there missed opportunities to amplify key moments into scenes? Is the language sharp or in need of revisiting?

As a feedback provider, I feel responsible for attending to these kinds of narrative issues. As a human, I feel awful just writing those cold words.

I am fortunate to know that particular mother who shared the story of her daughter's accidental death. For several years she workshopped her memoir in my classes, and she is now in the process of crafting a query letter to agents. A few months ago she shared an early draft of her query with the group, which describes seeing her little girl lying on an adult-size gurney in the hospital—the familiar wisp of her blond cowlick, the purplish tint of her lips, her Looney Tunes hospital gown several sizes too large, plus myriad other details filling two paragraphs.

"I think you might want to cut the opening paragraphs by half," I heard myself say, not as someone who has long been inspired by this woman's courage as a writer and human being, and not as a mother myself who can't even begin to fathom the pain of losing a child, but as a professional editor who knows when something feels overwritten to the detriment of clarity and the author's purpose. "The impact of that moment feels blunted by too many details."

"I think you're right," the woman responded, with no hint of defensiveness or dramatics. If she could keep it together as we talked about those paragraphs, then who was I to let emotion override my editorial instincts?

The next week, the woman returned to our class with a revised draft of her query letter. In the revision, she had selectively honed down the two opening paragraphs to one brutal scenic moment. It turns out I had given her good advice, for better or worse, because with that shorter, sharper opening, I could see even more clearly that little girl in her oversized Looney Tunes hospital gown, the purplish tint to her lips, her wisp of a cowlick. In fact, I can still see her now.

Five Tips for Critiquing a Sad Story

1. How can you not feel for a writer when the subject of her story is heartbreaking? "I'm so sorry." "How are you holding up?" "Life can be so unfair." Sympathetic comments to a one, but consider that the writer may see her critique group as a welcome opportunity to *not* talk about her feelings and simply focus on her work. As such, assume this writer, like any participant in the group, is not looking for sympathy so much as quality feedback.

2. As just noted, a story discussion—even when the material is difficult—should remain focused on narrative issues, but that doesn't mean you have to behave like a sea cucumber. In advance of the critique, acknowledge the painful subject matter. Share your appreciation of the strength it took for the writer to revisit her trauma. Practice being both human and a feedback provider at the same time, which is actually good advice when critiquing any kind of story.

3. Imagine a world, or a workshop, where people didn't have empathy. No thanks. But when cognitive empathy (the capacity to take on another person's perspective and understand their feelings) shifts too far in the direction of emotional empathy (meaning we are actually feeling the same distress as the person in pain), the feedback provider's weep-a-thon can quickly become a distraction. When working with someone writing about a difficult experience, beware you don't become engrossed in your own emotions. Your job is to keep it together enough to respond to the writing. Otherwise who is helping whom?

4. Speak up, even if you are hesitant. You are not being unkind by pointing out areas in the text that would be served by revision. Similarly, you are not being crass by appreciating the craft that contributed to the power of the prose.

5. Avoid discussion drift. Any good story serves as fodder for all sorts of compelling conversations. I recently was in a workshop, for example, where we were supposed to be critiquing a chapter of a historical novel set in Scotland, yet somehow we detoured into a long discussion about how we should all take a trip to Orkney to see the stone circles. Obviously, a memoir about a tragedy doesn't invoke vacation planning, but it can lead to participants sharing their own stories of grief and loss, leaving little time or energy for critiquing the submitted pages.

Four Breaths In. Four Breaths Out.

SMALL MIRACLES

Maybe because I am a writer, and because I'm the opposite of intimidating to anyone who meets me, people are always asking me for feedback on their stories, book proposals, articles, and even cover letters for job applications, though I haven't had an office job for years. Usually I say yes, partly because I have run up so much karmic debt that I am afraid to say no. What if I bring on some cosmic curse by selfishly refusing to help others, especially after all the help I have been given with my own writing? But the other reason I am willing to give people feedback is because it makes me feel really, really powerful.

Writers care what you think about their writing. They care more than you can sometimes fathom, unless you are a writer yourself, of course. Here is what I mean. Tell a person they're a bad driver and they don't start agonizing over whether they should turn in their license. They just keep on merrily sideswiping mailboxes and going forty in the passing lane. But tell the same person they're a bad writer and they're apt to go to pieces, or maybe even quit writing forever—which is strange when you think about it, since bad writing, as opposed to bad driving, doesn't endanger innocent lives.

It's heady having that kind of power.

As I was working on this book, I invited almost every writer I encountered to tell me about their experiences with feedback. Even I was surprised by how much emotion this subject evoked; how big a role feedback plays in writers' lives, whether they are new to the craft or have been publishing for years. Non-writers, too, have their own share of defining feedback moments. Years ago, I met a ninety-one-year-old man at a book party. He had spent his entire adult life working for the railroad, yet the first thing he told me after we were introduced was how he had won a high school play-writing contest back in 1931. "The prize money was twenty-five dollars," he tapped his cane for emphasis. "You'd better believe, that was a lot of money during the Depression."

In the introduction to this book, I wrote that almost every writer has a toxic feedback story; how somebody's ill-considered, insensitive, or just plain wrongheaded feedback undermined their writing or their confidence. Here, I would like to add that the opposite is equally true; just as many writers have stories about a particular someone whose feedback encouraged or sustained them along the way.

One of these stories belongs to Teresa Lust, the author of *Pass the Polenta and Other Writings from the Kitchen,* a memoir and cookbook inspired by her childhood family meals and her experiences as a professional cook. When Teresa was getting her master's degree in liberal studies at Dartmouth College, she was too intimidated to sign up for any of the writing courses offered in the program. "I thought, *If I can't do it, I'll be crushed,*" she said. Teresa did, however, enroll in an environmental studies class taught by Noel Perrin, an English professor who drove what was probably one of the world's first solar cars and was the author of numerous acclaimed essays and books about his experiences with rural life. Teresa's first assignment in the class was to write a paper on anything that pertained to the journey of Lewis and Clark. She wrote about the endangered salmon habitat at the mouth of the Columbia River, where Lewis and Clark spent the winter of 1805 and where Teresa had worked her first kitchen job. When Professor Perrin returned Teresa's paper to her, his feedback took her by surprise. "You're a writer," he told her, which she automatically denied. "Well," he countered in his amiable way, "if you don't think of yourself as one, then you won't be."

From this brief bit of feedback came a "small miracle," as Teresa put it. To be a writer, she realized, you have to stop worrying about whether other people are more qualified than you, or whether you will be any good. You just have to write. Noel Perrin's feedback motivated Teresa to enroll in her first writing course, a Dartmouth class in creative nonfiction. The echo of her professor's encouragement also gave her the courage to write about what mattered to her—food and family.

The first essay Teresa submitted to the class for review described how her German grandmother had taught her to make pie dough. Witnessing the quality and content of the pieces the class discussed before hers, Teresa grew increasingly nervous about her own submission. "I thought I should be writing about world history, or synapses, or something more sophisticated,"

Teresa explains, "but at the same time I felt I expressed my heart." To her relief, the feedback process was "very positive," she said. "It wasn't that they told me, 'Don't change a word,' but they liked what I was writing, and they gave me feedback that helped crystallize what I wanted to say."

Teresa's essay, "Easy as Pie," marked the start of a collection of food-related anecdotes and recipes that evolved into her master's thesis and ultimately earned her a publishing contract before she had even finished her graduate program. After Teresa's book came out from Steerforth Press, a reviewer in the *Washington Post* wrote, "Of the many cookbooks-as-memoirs to appear in recent years, the one I like best is Teresa Lust's *Pass the Polenta and Other Writings from the Kitchen,* a beautiful collection of essays by a one-time professional chef who cooks not for money but for love." Teresa happened upon this review, which was part of a longer article about several books within the same genre, when the piece was picked up by her local newspaper. When she read the reference to *Pass the Polenta* her immediate response was, *Oh no, someone else wrote a book with my same title!* Then it registered—the praise was for her.

Noel Perrin wasn't the only feedback provider who helped Teresa on her progression from insecure graduate student to published writer. In the acknowledgments of her book, Teresa also thanks her thesis advisor and her writing group, which evolved from the class where she timidly submitted her first essay. But Teresa's story exemplifies a lovely truth. Sometimes it only takes one person to help a writer on her way; to change the course of a writing life. For Teresa, that person was Noel Perrin.

For another writer, it could be you.

I once read an article on leadership that stated that we all influence 250 people in our lifetime. That number strikes me as conservative, especially if one of your roles in life is that of a feedback provider for writers. A few words of honest encouragement, a thoughtful response to a manuscript, a few hours of your time . . . What may seem like a small effort on your part may resonate with the writer more than you know. Think about this the next time someone asks you to comment on their writing. Think about your own feedback stories and the particular someones who have been instrumental in your writing life. As a feedback provider, you have the opportunity to replenish the good karma. It is in your power to make a positive difference. You could be a writer's small miracle.

PATRICK MADDEN: "I DEFINITELY FOUND IN MYSELF A RELUCTANCE TO MESS WITH TOO MUCH."

Once a physics major, Patrick Madden often heard that he was good at math and science. "I loved that," he says, "because it played really well into my worldview. I wanted things to be firm and clear and defined." Now, however, Patrick, the author of three acclaimed essay collections, whose work has been noted in nine volumes of *The Best American Essays,* sees that worldview as somewhat adolescent. "My educational journey has shifted," he shares, "away from a desire for certainty to an appreciation for the richness of ambiguities. And I think that's what essaying does."

As a creative-writing professor at Brigham Young University and the Vermont College of Fine Arts, Patrick now sees that same desire for certainty in many of his undergraduate and MFA students. To help them shift from binary thinking and the comfort of conclusions, he encourages them not just to essay (a word derived from the French infinitive *essayer,* "to try" or "to attempt") toward a particular piece of writing, but to essay through life, attuned to the world's delights and calamities.

On paper and in the real world, Patrick encourages this sense of discovery, in part by giving some assignments that purposely will *not* be critiqued because, as he puts it, "students' work is often really good when they can just play at writing and experiment, without worrying that anybody is going to tell them to change it." Patrick also admits that students have to work hard to *not* get an A in his class.

When students' drafts are being workshopped, he prompts the discussions with open-ended questions—How did this strike you? At what point in the piece did you begin to pick up on the author's theme or central idea? "I do always have things to say," Patrick adds, "things I think will be valuable to the writer's revisions. But I also don't want students to feel like they're just in class to hear Pat opine on what they should do or 'fix.'" He believes the goal of a workshop is to not tell the writer what to do, but to offer responses to the work, so the writer can see how a piece lands in the minds of different readers. Patrick also reminds his students that, to a large degree, a writer can't control the meaning of a work. "We can hope to shape and convey certain things, but the experience of reading a piece will always be informed by what the reader brings to it."

Readers of Patrick's own award-winning essay collections are likely to experience them in myriad ways. From his debut, *Quotidiana,* to his more recent work, *Disparates,* his essays have been described as ingenuous, erudite, a generous romp, rich in wordplay . . . Particularly appreciative are students and teachers of the traditions and tenets of the form, who celebrate Patrick's often experimental approach and ability to find new opportunities within the genre—and this from a man once inclined toward certainty.

When I invited Patrick to share with me his thoughts on writing, teaching, and feedback, what transpired was a leisurely conversation that, in a way, mimicked his advice for drafting an essay—take your time, be open to discovery, go down the paths of interest. Somewhere in the conversation, I asked him, "In your own writing past, can you recall a particular moment or interaction where you experienced the magic of the feedback process?" What follows is his response.

> One of my colleagues, Joey Franklin, was a student in one of the very first workshops I ever taught when I started at Brigham Young University. He was an undergraduate when I encountered him and certainly a good writer, but the thing I noticed about him, that set him apart from everybody else, was that he would revise voraciously. His drafts changed so much that you couldn't easily tell that what you were reading was a revision of the thing you had read before.
>
> Basically, the pieces he handed out in class were just an opening to access the thing he was exploring in the background. And when he heard our feedback—where we were engaged, where he lost us, where we thought he might want to look at a related concept—he would go back not to the thing on the paper, but to the thing behind the paper, which had now gathered all sorts of different, interesting companions. And that's how he became a really fine writer.

Now, I don't think this is always necessary. Sometimes you can write a pretty good first draft that just requires a little polish. But early on as a writer, I definitely found in myself a reluctance to mess with too much. When I wrote something, I only wanted somebody to tell me what punctuation I needed. But Joey taught me to truly think differently about feedback and revision.

Joey's been my colleague for about ten years now, and recently I brought him one of my pieces called "Unpredictable Essays." It was created by feeding my first two books into a predictive-text-bot program. This provided me with an array of twenty or so words to choose from my own work, and I would just click through them, and with each word I clicked, it provided me with a new matrix of suggested words, just like what happens with your phone, except your phone has three suggested words and this had twenty-something.

That's how I wrote the original essay, ten paragraphs' worth of weird, somewhat aphoristic, nonsensical stuff. Then I gave it to Joey, and the two of us workshopped it, and he said, "This is interesting, but it doesn't make any sense. I don't get it." And, I think accessing his own kind of revisionary attitudes, he suggested, "Why not footnote each paragraph and, in the footnote, don't use predictive text, just allow yourself to write explanatorily, but also creatively."

And that was it. After that advice, I went back and more than doubled the length of the piece, and it became an essay that I'm still proud of, an essay that's cool in the weird, predictive-text gobble-dygook way, but it also grounds itself by allowing the footnotes to explore concepts of hybridity, autonomy, regurgitation, self-exploration, the participatory universe.

I'm not trying to brag about my own essay, but just to say that the initial idea was just weird. But in workshopping it with Joey, whose ideas about revision are quite drastic at times, I could make the essay into something that actually works.

"Who wants to share first?"

HEY, LET'S PUT ON A WORKSHOP!

You tried a writer's meet-up advertised on a flyer on the wall of the health-food store, but it turned out to be more of a support group for aging hippies. You took a community college course on fiction writing, but now that you've passed with a B-plus you feel it's time to move on. The online class you took was really inspiring, but it was lecture based and left you hungering for more deadlines and input on your own work. And while your wife says she is willing to critique your work, the only feedback she offered on the last story you gave her was, "Do you really think I talk too much, like the wife in the story?"

So where can you turn to for the kind of ongoing insights, camaraderie, and deadlines you crave during the often long and lonely creative process?

How about starting your own writing workshop or critique group? (Here I am using those terms interchangeably, though a workshop is often facilitated by an instructor, whereas a critique group typically consists of peers.) Starting my own workshop—with me as the teacher/facilitator—was exactly what I did way back when I found myself in need of a writing community after moving from Minneapolis to small-town New England, where legend had it the woods were filled with writers, but none of them seemed to congregate except at nearby Dartmouth College or at the general store.

Looking back, I can now see this as a bold move; bold in that I had recently finished a master's program at Dartmouth focused on creative writing, but I had few teaching credentials at the time. Go for it anyway, I thought, because I had been a narrative-craft wonk for years (just the thought of muscle verbs and scenic detail and objective correlatives makes me passionate), plus one of the best things about a workshop or any writing group is that everyone plays a teaching role. We would all be learning from one another.

Add to that the fact that I was suffering from serious workshop withdrawal, particularly the kind of community workshops I experienced in Minneapolis, home of the Loft Literary Center. Founded in 1974 above a bookstore, the Loft offers a cornucopia of workshops and programs for whatever genre or aspect of writing you are into. When I lived in Minneapolis, I took back-to-back creative-writing classes, most of them from an instructor who came from England and used to play rugby. I didn't know much about his teaching credentials, but I loved his accent, and my skills and confidence improved. After our weekly meetings, the whole class would go out drinking and flirt and bitch about how hard it was to be a writer. Those were the good old days, at least from what I can remember.

Except for the drinking, flirting, and bitching part, the writing workshop I started in Vermont was modeled in large part by those classes I took at the Loft. Since leading my first workshop a couple decades ago, some fundamental things have not changed, in terms of what I see as the most productive way to foster learning and supportive group dynamics. What has changed is that I no longer teach from a back room of my house, a room furnished with little more than green plastic chairs and a Foosball table. In those early days, I remember having a big pot of soup available for those writers coming straight from work. I remember how my husband at the time did his best to contain our little girls and incontinent dog to the rest of the house. I also remember thinking this was the best job in the world—teaching the craft of writing—and that is another thing that has not changed.

As my teaching practice grew, I moved my workshop out of my home and founded my own Writer's Center, offering in-person and online classes. I also began teaching at a diversity of academic institutions, including Dartmouth and other graduate programs, and at writing conferences, libraries, and social-services organizations. Sometimes I and some of the original participants from the Back Room Workshop will wax nostalgic about the old days when we gathered on my plastic chairs to coax each other along. That said, other than the lack of soup and the pitter patter of little feet overhead, I think that homey spirit has carried through to all of my workshops. It no longer surprises me that even a workshop over Zoom can create a true sense of community and foster close friendships, if it is done right.

If you would like to start a workshop or writing group, all you really need is a back room of your own, if not in your house, then maybe in a private room in the public library, or a corner of a bookstore café, or online. The logistics are simple. You will want to allow about two hours per gathering, enough time to accommodate both a meaningful agenda and the attention span of adults who have to be up at 6:00 the next morning to face their nonwriting lives. I recommend holding your workshop on Thursday evenings, since everyone seems to be doing something else on Wednesday nights. Of course, morning meetings are just as good, so whatever works for your schedule is fine.

My workshops vary in length from four to eight weeks. Having an end date to the workshop strengthens the commitment among members because they know from the outset that their participation is time-limited. It also allows for a more graceful disbanding—no lingering demise as members drift away. Writers who are interested in continuing can always sign up for the next session, and the next, and the next . . . In my classes, at least half the participants are returning members, eager to learn more, enjoy the camaraderie of their fellow writers, or finish full drafts or revisions of their works-in-progress.

When I first started advertising my workshop, I was lucky if three people were willing to sign up for a writing group at the house of a strange woman, who may be a close talker or a flake. Nevertheless, even with those initial small numbers, we did good work and had fun. That said, I think the ideal size for a workshop is anywhere from five to eight participants. In either extreme, the group is large enough to offer a range of opinions and maybe even a consensus, but small enough to feel close-knit.

Some workshops qualify members through writing samples, but I love the idea of a true community workshop that gives everyone permission to try creative writing. So many times a novice who arrives at class with no immediate display of talent ends up being one of the workshop gems. I also find great value in diversity. It gives me hope for all of humanity when I see advanced writers and neophytes, writers of genre and literary fiction, and aspiring authors with different voices from different cultures intermingling in the same workshop, breaking down barriers as they learn how to critique and appreciate each other's work.

One of the biggest challenges of a writing group is to help people overcome their nervousness about sharing their work. To alleviate this fear as quickly as possible, I often start the meetings with a timed prompt or writing exercise. Good prompts are all around us; you need only look up and react to the first thing that catches your eye. Of course, the beauty of a prompt is that there is no wrong way to respond, other than to refuse to move the pen.

Most of the meeting time is spent reviewing participants' pages, with each writer getting opportunities to submit something for formal review as many times as possible. In my groups, submissions range from barely disguised notes to revisions of revisions; in other words, they run the gamut of the creative process. We welcome all sincere efforts and meet every draft where it

Hey, Let's Put On a Workshop!

currently stands, whether it is a standalone piece or an excerpt from a longer work. The only parameter is that writers submit something they genuinely want to develop or polish.

Participants use the days before each meeting to swap pages and ready their critiques. I suggest everyone read each submission at least two times, with the first read preferably done in the bathtub, without a red pen. This perusal is for pleasure and first impressions; the second read is to scrutinize the text as a workshopper, which is likely to cause you to be hypercritical. That's okay, though, because you can always weigh your harsher judgments against your first impressions. Are you simply looking for problems? Or is something truly problematic?

A good discussion of, say, an eight-page submission takes somewhere between fifteen to forty-five minutes, depending on its issues. Less time means the group probably isn't giving the work its full due. More time means the group is likely rehashing the same points to death. The manuscript dictates what aspects of the piece deserve the most attention—characterization, plot, voice, detail, pacing, dialogue, prose rhythm, language, even punctuation in some cases, if the story only needs polishing. On the other hand, if the submission is a super-rough draft or represents more a collection of ideas or notes, the discussion should be geared toward pointing out areas for development or amplification.

A common misconception among workshop members is that the story discussion only benefits the writer. No way! Every discussion illuminates valuable lessons about craft and the creative process that apply to every writer in the room.

That's about all there is to putting on a workshop, though of course I am being simplistic. A successful writing group or workshop takes continual effort, but the rewards far outweigh the challenges. A good workshop gives you access to a diversity of reading talents, since some members will be good at critiquing plot; others, good copy editors; and others, confidence boosters. Plus, a writing group not only teaches you how to write, but how to be a writer. This communal experience helps you see the world through a writer's eyes, to notice and listen as a writer, and to read as a writer. Last, but hardly least, participating in such a meaningful, communal experience helps us polish our communication skills and offers us practice at being decent human beings.

How will you know if your workshop is successful? In my case, I think of something Carole, a participant who has taken the workshop several times, told me the week after a chapter from her young-adult novel was critiqued. On the drive home that cold autumn night, Carole felt compelled to roll down all the car windows, let the wind stream through her long, brown hair, and put the pedal to the metal. That was how charged up she felt to get back to her writing desk and go at it again. And that is how you will know if your workshop is successful.

Sample In-Person Workshop Itinerary

6:30 p.m. Writers claim their seats. Important! Once a writer stakes out a chair at the first meeting, he "owns" that seat for the rest of the workshop. Writers hate disruption of their personal habits, so even if you are the first to arrive at subsequent meetings, do not try to move in on someone else's space. (I'm only partially kidding here.)

6:30–6:45 p.m. If meeting in person at someone's home, consider serving coffee and cheap, store-bought cookies to provide a sense of hominess and a sugar high without creating the expectation that you will be baking every week. Share writing news. Who faced what writing challenges that week? Who triumphed? Did anyone learn or read or hear anything relevant to writing?

6:45–7:00 p.m. Group writing exercise. Inevitably, certain members will gripe about this and claim they can't write anything good under this kind of time pressure. Ignore their whining and make sure to congratulate them later when they do, indeed, write something good, which will always be the case, if not that evening, then the next.

7:00–8:30 p.m. Discussion of the pages submitted for review. Decide ahead whether all feedback will be verbal or a combination of verbal and written. Also, decide how many participants' work will be up for discussion per meeting. I feel the more deadlines the better, so I invite everyone to submit every week, which limits the number of pages shared to about three to six or so, but still allows us to help each participant write forward in small but steady increments. (Many groups limit the number of discussions per meeting but allow for longer submissions. Do what's preferable for the majority of your group members.)

8:30–8:45 p.m. End the meeting fifteen to twenty minutes late. I have no idea how to avoid this, so perhaps you could let me know if your group manages to finish on time.

Postscript: Fifteen-Minute Miracles

In years of leading workshops, I have invented thousands of writing prompts, and they always make me look good. Not because the prompts themselves are remarkable, but because when people commit to moving the pen and trusting the process during a timed writing exercise, something wonderful almost always results, whether it's the curious nature of word association or the miracle of a perfectly formed story in a first draft, which happens more often than I can get my head around.

In my groups, I strongly encourage participants to share their responses to the prompt aloud, not for critique but for appreciation. This also allows us to bear witness to something we rarely if ever get to experience with our fellow writers: the very origins of another writer's creative process. Guaranteed, you will be gobsmacked by the quality of much of the writing. But more often than not, no one is more surprised than the writer herself to see what has emerged on the page—images, characters, entire scenes she had no idea had been tucked inside her.

Below are just a few examples of prompts that have proven themselves useful, no matter how the writer responds to them.

An intriguing line of dialogue. "Meet me at 3:00 a.m." "Is this seat taken?" "Thanks, but no thanks." The beauty of offering a suggestive line of dialogue is that it often leads to the writer immediately immersing himself in a scenic moment. That said, I've seen responses to this type of prompt where the writer ends up using that line as the perfect conclusion to a scene or even an entire story, as if he'd planned it all along. Amazing!

Lists. Another way to nudge along the creative process, especially if participants are feeling uncreative or particularly anxious, is to invite everyone to make a list of the contents of their bedside drawer, or what they would save in the case of a fire, or their most memorable meals. You get the idea. Because list-making is something many of us do daily, it's non-threatening yet fruitful in mining meaningful material. Part two of this same exercise is to pick just one item from the list, whichever one catches your eye, and expand on it.

Epistles. Yet another type of prompt that serves as an easy "in" is to ask participants to write a letter (or email, text, or voicemail) to one of the characters in their story, or to a person from their own past. Because the epistolary form is such a familiar way to communicate, it's also an effective way to help writers start writing.

Everyday objects. As William Carlos Williams famously said, "No ideas but in things." In other words, writing about a simple object (a travel mug, a tube of pink lipstick, a dog collar) can quickly evoke much deeper content as the writer begins to form associations and make thematic leaps.

THE MYTH OF THE SAFE SPACE

The second-floor reading room in the local library accommodates a few over-stuffed chairs, two rockers, and a loveseat, all arranged in a lopsided circle. It's midsummer and the room is stuffy, even with the windows open. The poetry circle that meets here once a month to write and share their work is about to begin; eight of the seats are filled with mostly women and a few men.

The facilitator, let's call him Peter, warmly greets each participant. Some are familiar faces who regularly attend this free and open-to-all gathering, and a few are newcomers to the circle. Peter's job is to offer a writing prompt and facilitate the poetry critiques that follow, but, equally important, he is charged with creating a safe atmosphere for every participant. No one would ever accuse Peter of fostering anything but a welcoming environment, but of course in any group people arrive with psychological baggage.

"I need you to stop doing that," a newcomer confronts the fiftyish woman in the rocker next to her. The newcomer is clearly agitated. She pulls at the threads of her sweater sleeves.

"Stop doing what?" the woman in the rocker asks. All she was doing was fanning herself with her notebook, trying to mitigate another one of her hot flashes.

"That!" the newcomer points to the makeshift fan that her neighbor continues to move slowly back and forth in front of her flushed face. "It's a trigger for me, and I don't feel safe."

The woman in the rocker is taken aback. For three years she has been coming to this circle. The people who show up each month are all so nice that she hardly ever gets nervous anymore when she shares her poems. But now, this newcomer has made her feel embarrassed and, yes, angry. Tears spring to her eyes, an overreaction she can't seem to stop. She feels like she is being accused of something—insensitivity or ignorance—and gathers her things to leave.

Peter catches her by the door, and after a brief, whispered conversation he convinces her to return to her rocker. Quickly, he starts the meeting by offering the group a writing prompt. After that, things progress as usual, thank goodness. But once again, as the facilitator of the workshop, he is reminded of the myth of the safe space. No matter how welcoming the group, certain actions—even those that may seem innocuous—can act as emotional triggers.

In life and in writing groups, emotional triggers are everywhere—memories, experiences, actions, particular words—that, by association, cause people with a history of trauma to experience strong feelings of anxiety. (Note the distinction between being triggered, which causes someone to feel as if they are reliving the trauma, versus discomfort about something that rubs someone the wrong way.) There are some subjects—domestic violence and racial tension, for example—that are more predictable triggers, but as the example with the fan demonstrates (which was a true story, save for a few minor details), there is no way to anticipate all the forms that triggers can take.

Now add to this challenge the realities of a writing workshop, where story material rife with traumatic situations is often the fodder for discussion. In such circumstances, it seems almost inevitable that someone will feel triggered at one point or another, while others may feel wrongly accused of insensitivity or even feel like they are the ones being victimized when someone else plays the non-safe card.

Despite these challenges, there are ways to foster a workshop environment that minimizes emotional triggers or helps address the situation with grace and understanding. Below are a few guidelines to help make everyone not only feel more secure, but welcome.

- If you are going to be sharing difficult content, give the group a heads up.
- Allow those who feel triggered to pass on responding to material that makes them uncomfortable.
- Be aware that what feels like a safe space for the majority members of the group may not feel the same for someone in the minority.
- Show respect and a willingness to learn from participants experiencing the aftermath of trauma.

• Practice compassionate listening. Often we can best be in service not by reacting or even responding, but by simply allowing the person feeling unsafe to be heard.

• In my own writer's center, there is a small poster that says, "Non-Judgment Day is here." It's a good reminder for me and the others to not be critical of other people's emotional insecurities or sensitivities.

GREGORY MAGUIRE: "I DON'T REVISE IN AN ARCHITECTURAL WAY."

Envision yourself as an imaginative, high-energy boy growing up in a restrictive, Irish Catholic household. Money is tight and television is forbidden, with the exception of the one movie your parents allow you and your six siblings to watch once a year—*The Wizard of Oz.* How do you overcome your feelings of boredom and confinement without getting yourself into trouble? If you're Gregory Maguire, you read, read, read, and you teach yourself how to write stories. Indeed, Gregory proved himself such a good teacher, he went on to become the author of several dozen crossover books for adults and children, including the best seller *Wicked: The Life and Times of the Wicked Witch of the West,* which became a blockbuster Broadway musical.

As a kid, Gregory wrote hundreds of stories, but rewriting, said the author, wasn't part of the process. "My method was to keep working, keep spewing, not go back and fix things up. I rarely crossed out a word or changed a paragraph. If I reread something and didn't like it, I figured I'd just do it better the next time." In fact, the only thing Gregory was less interested in than rewriting was getting feedback on his stories. "I only cared about my own satisfaction," he explained. "I wrote and illustrated for an audience of one."

Gregory was twenty-three when he first received feedback, after submitting a fantasy novel for children to Farrar, Straus & Giroux. He was encouraged when the editor asked him to meet with her, until he saw his manuscript on her desk. "The pages were edged with so many Post-it notes it looked like a hedgehog in epileptic shock." Page by page, the editor walked him through her comments on pacing, character inconsistencies, errors in grammar, etc. "This terrified me," Gregory said, "but I sat through three and a half hours of this exercise because I figured she was going to offer me a contract."

Instead, the editor closed the meeting by handing him back his heavily edited manuscript. She told him that if he made the effort to revise, he could resubmit the novel. Otherwise, try another publisher. "This was in the days before personal computers, and that marked-up manuscript was my only copy," Gregory offered with a laugh. "I had no choice but to redo it." Four months later, he turned in a significantly revised version of *The Lightning Time,* which Farrar published in 1978.

"It's taken me twenty-five years to get used to the feedback process," Gregory revealed, "and I'm still not always a gracious receiver of critical comment." In his early twenties, he did join a writer's group, but he only lasted for two sessions. He was turned off by the group's "micromanaging syllables" and uncomfortable with any discussions about the moral reasons for a story to exist. "I knew myself well enough to know that if I let anyone question a particular phrase or turn of events in my story, I could become paralyzed. I was only interested in productivity." A writer who describes himself as "colossally self-motivated," he still prefers to hang on to his work until he thinks it is finished. "But for all I say I've taught myself to write without feedback," Gregory admitted, "I do need it."

Over the years, Gregory has "cobbled together" a band of three or four feedback providers, including his editor at HarperCollins, his artist spouse, and his brother Joe, a mathematician whom Gregory often turns to when he is in a narrative pinch. For example, when Gregory was writing his fourth novel, *Mirror, Mirror* (2003), a revision of *Snow White,* he decided a change of focus would help stimulate his thinking about the dwarves. So he asked his brother to explain the different properties of the numbers seven and eight. After hearing Joe talk about eight being a complex number (divisible in many ways) as opposed to the prime number seven, the author found the narrative structure he had been seeking. In the book, the dwarves start out as a "stable constellation" of eight, but when one goes on a journey, everything changes.

Asked if he has grown more willing to revise than in the early days, Gregory answered with a conditional yes. When he was completing his new novel, *Son of a Witch,* for example, he wasn't confident about one of his female characters, so he asked for feedback from two men and two women. The male readers thought the character worked fine, but one of the women found her inconsistent and didn't believe her actions at the end. "Since that was my sneaking suspicion anyway, that's the reader I listened to," he said.

"I don't revise in an architectural way," Gregory added, "because I don't start something until I feel confident in the framework, and I devise the structure as a larger metaphor for the theme of the book. People have never said to me, 'Make the ending the beginning,' or, 'Bring in the dancing girls in chapter 4.' I couldn't do that," he explained. "If I have to bulldoze, I'm not interested in doing it again. The structure is what it is. It's concrete," the author asserted, "but I will move the furniture around the room."

Gregory Maguire

HOW TO HAVE A GOOD
GROUP DISCUSSION

Have you ever been in a workshop when a submission comes up for review and a silence falls over the group? Not the kind of silence that feels like people are gathering their thoughts, or reliving the sex they wish they'd had last night, but the kind of silence that implies no one can think of anything remotely useful or good to say about the work. At least that is how it feels to the writer, who is sitting there wishing she could disappear between the floorboards. Meanwhile, the other group members are avoiding eye contact by staring at the toes of their damp wool socks peeking out from their Birkenstock sandals (if it is winter in Vermont). Some of them really can't think of anything good to say. Others aren't sure what they are supposed to say. And some members just don't want to be the first one to say anything because they're afraid they might say something foolish.

Why wouldn't this happen in a writing group? Group dynamics can be weird under any circumstances, but when a group has the emotionally charged agenda of helping writers improve their writing, that is bound to make things even weirder, especially since the whole workshop scenario is a bit of a setup. A writer submits his work for criticism, which can make everyone else in the group feel pressured into criticizing it, which can make the writer feel lousy. And to make matters worse, you personally could be the culprit! You could be the villain in someone else's toxic-feedback story, even though you are only there to be helpful.

The good news is, it is possible to alleviate the tentativeness, awkwardness, and negativity that place a pall over so many group discussions (and one-on-one feedback interactions). What follows are some suggestions on how your group can foster a feedback session that is both productive and positive. I promise you, there is always something good to talk about in every submission, and there is always a way to offer criticism in a way that is both constructive and even motivating. I know this for a fact, having participated in hundreds of workshop discussions. What I don't know, after all these years, is why anyone in their right mind would wear socks with sandals, *especially* if it is winter in Vermont.

Take every submission seriously. Writers don't submit anything frivolously; too much is at stake, emotionally speaking. What may look to you like a dashed-off piece or a scant few pages may represent a world of effort on the writer's part. As workshop participants, it is not our place to judge the worthiness of someone else's submission. If it matters to the writer, it matters.

Meet the story where it's at. Is the submission a first or fifth draft? Is the writer looking for a general response or line edits? This kind of information can help you tailor your feedback appropriately. Think of it this way: You don't fault a baby for not being an adult. If the writer's submission is in the early stages of development, you will want to focus your feedback on the piece's potential rather than its lack of sophistication. Conversely, if a mature work is presented, you will be doing the writer a favor by pointing out any lingering traces of babbling or self-indulgence that undermine the story's refinement.

Beware the HIPPO effect. The HIPPO effect is a term borrowed from business that suggests that once the highest-paid person at the meeting gives their opinion, others are more likely to jump on the bandwagon. This effect undermines individual thought and can silence voices. In a writing group, salaries aren't so much the issue, but the power dynamic can be thrown off if, for example, the facilitator or the "best" writer in the group always sounds in loud and first. And this effect is amplified for the minorities in a group, say the only woman of color in a team dominated by white men, or the only introvert in a group of extroverts, or the only unpublished writer in a group of seasoned authors. To avoid this kind of subversion and/or conformity, make sure to advocate for your own ideas (don't hesitate to speak up, for example, for fear of sounding like an idiot or outlier), and do your part to invite a diversity of ideas and perspectives.

Distinguish between "this reader" and "readers." Beware of assuming that your opinion mirrors the opinions of the rest of the reading public. For example, comments like, "Readers will never believe your protagonist is an international art thief . . ." or, "No one wants to read stories about friendly vampires . . ." assign you an authority that is not yours to assume, and that is, frankly, obnoxious. Yes, you are entitled to your opinion and can share strong views, but typically writers, or rather *this writer,* would prefer you speak for yourself and leave the gross generalizations out of your critique.

Invite the writer to do a mini-reading. Before launching into the discussion, invite the writer to read a few paragraphs aloud. This lends dignity to the submission. It also magnifies a work's strengths and glitches and allows you to pick up on nuances of voice or other aspects of the writing that you may have missed when you read it silently. If you think a piece works better read aloud, it probably means the inflections, pacing, and emotions the writer is bringing to the read need to be reinforced on the page.

Be up. It's important to create as much positive energy as commentary because the latter without the former can leave the writer nonplussed. *Geez,* the writer leaves the meeting thinking, They told me they liked my story, but then why didn't anyone act like it? As every writer knows, showing can be a lot more effective than telling, especially when it comes to enthusiasm.

Start with praise. Why make things harder than they have to be? Start the session by talking about what you like in the piece and why. Here is an example: "I like how the character of the grandma swats flies while she is canning, and her sweat drips into the preserves. Those details really showed the heat of the kitchen and the old woman's perseverance." Starting with praise makes the writer feel good (for good reason) and gives her the perspective she needs to counterbalance any critical remarks that follow. It's a lot easier on you, too.

What do you notice? Telling the writer what you noticed in the text is another terrific way to launch the discussion, especially if you are having trouble coming up with something you liked about the piece. "I noticed the alliteration in the first stanza." "I noticed the father was absent for most of the story." "I noticed that the part of the story from the aunt's perspective was written in the past tense, and the part of the story from the niece's perspective was written in the present tense." These observations may seem small, but they are useful because they tell the writer what aspects of the writing are drawing your attention, for better or for worse.

What's not wrong? Way too many writing teachers and workshop peers still harbor the misguided notion that the only way to help others (and ourselves) write forward productively is to hone in on a text's deficits, to the degree we willfully ignore what is actually working on the page. But this singular perspective is warped and counterproductive, not just because relentless negativity can feel overwhelming and cause editorial paralysis, but also because it fails to provide perspective. In contrast, by making a point to illuminate what's *not* wrong in the text, an approach borrowed from Thich Nhat Hanh's teachings from *Peace Is Every Step,* you help the writer discern what to keep as well as what to model as they generate more pages or revise.

Keep in mind, writing is not the same as doing math. As a discipline, creative writing is not the same as solving an equation, so let go of a binary mindset. There are no wrong answers, per se, when critiquing, and there is no one right answer. (For that matter, there is no definitive indicator to signify your story is finished, so you can let go of that notion as well.) Much of what makes a story or poem work or not work is found in the gray areas; thus while binary thinking may help us feel a sense of certainty, the art of writing demands we feel equally comfortable with a degree of uncertainty. In the end, after you've exhausted craft and all your feedback providers have gone home, all you can do is trust your own instincts when it comes to revision or deciding whether your work is done.

Critique in a continuum. Good dog! Bad dog! Maybe you need to be that definitive when training Trixie the Wonder Dog, but writers respond better when feedback is part of a continuum (not working, almost working) rather than categories (good, bad). After all, would you rather hear, "I don't think your plot is working yet," or, "I think your plot is bad"? Incremental feedback softens the blow. More importantly, it helps the writer gauge how close he is to achieving his intent. It tells him whether he needs to rethink or refine.

Burst into reading. Think of your writing group as a movie musical. Just as the characters in a musical burst into song at opportune moments, you, too, can burst into the discussion by reading aloud your favorite sections. What better way to display your appreciation for a particular passage of writing, and pump up the energy of the workshop?

Turn suggestions into what ifs. Half the time writers resent suggestions, and half the time they glom on to them, which means you probably shouldn't make any, except it is so much fun (and useful at times). If the writer is open to suggestions, be sure yours have more to do with the writer's story than your own version of the writer's story. It is also helpful to phrase your suggestions as "what ifs" rather than declarations. Consider the difference between "Cut the opening!" and "The opening about the character's marital history didn't hook me. What if you filter all this background info into the story later?"

Go beyond yes-or-no questions. Say you ask your best friend, "Does this dress make me look fat?" If she says yes, you're crushed, and if she says no, you're happy; but what you don't know is that the fringe on the bodice makes you look like a wannabe for the Dallas Cowboys Cheerleaders, and the back of your hem is bunched up in your pantyhose. This speaks to the importance of asking open-ended questions in a story discussion—"What does everyone think about the ending?" "Why are you confused?" "How does the language affect the pacing?" Open-ended questions help stimulate the discussion and deliver useful insights that give the writer the whole story.

Take yourself out of it. Most How-to-Give-Feedback worksheets tell us to "own" our opinions by expressing them in terms of "I feel" or "I think." This makes sense, but you may want to ban the use of the "I" construct (at least temporarily) if it is limiting the depth of the constructive criticism. Notice the difference between "I think the diner waitress is really greedy" (the "I" construct makes it easy to stop after giving your opinion) versus "The waitress in the diner comes across as greedy to me because she steals the other waitress's tips." Another example: "I don't like the long flashback starting on page 2" versus "The long flashback starting on page 2 stopped the action right when it seemed to be picking up momentum."

Try different formats. Even if your group's existing format works just fine, it can be fun to experiment with new ones. Here are four options:

• Allow each feedback provider three minutes for his critique (yes, use a timer), then move on to an open discussion.
• Organize the discussion around four areas of critique: What is the piece about? What did you like about it? What didn't you like about it? How would you improve it?
• Only put forth positive feedback, not a word of constructive criticism.
• No written submissions; participants simply read aloud and follow up with verbal comments.

Show your appreciation. I still remember the first time a feedback provider thanked me for allowing her to read my submission. Somehow, this unexpected show of appreciation made me feel more like a "real" writer. It reminded me that even though my piece wasn't finished, my work already had value for the reader. I think the nicest way to close a group discussion is to say to the writer, "Thank you."

WHO'S IN CHARGE?

The worst writing group I was ever in consisted of six friends, all seasoned authors who also taught creative writing. You should have seen us, posturing and pontificating just to show how smart we were, feuding and fuming over each other's personality defects ("She always interrupts me when I'm talking!" "He never spends as much time on my stories as I spend on his!"), and defending our own stories to the bitter, bitter end. ("I *meant* to leave the reader confused!") The six of us exhibited every bad behavior imaginable in a critique group short of hair pulling, and don't think it didn't cross my mind.

Thankfully, we disbanded after a few months, and eventually most of us were restored to kinder, gentler relationships with each other, though I still avoid one member when I spot her at the grocery store. I often wondered why this effort was such a disaster, until one day the answer hit me—here we were, a writing group of teachers, yet nobody was leading the group.

Every writing group, without exception, needs someone to be in charge. This may be just my opinion, but on the other hand I know I am right, and not just from my own track record. I bet you have experienced your own share of failed groups, or you've heard stories, as I have, of writers who banded together to support each other's efforts only to suffer unhappy consequences. Likely these were good writers, and nice people, too—the kind of people who bring warm banana bread covered in gingham cloth to the meetings for everyone to share. Regardless, with no one at the helm, they quickly turned into the Jets and the Sharks, or fizzled out, or (worst of all) became a coffee klatch, an unpleasant-sounding term derived from the German word for "gossip." No wonder so many writers are suspicious of joining a group.

Here let me clarify an important point. When I refer to a group leader, I am not talking about a group tyrant. In fact, one of the first duties of the leader is to make sure the group runs like a democracy. As a whole, the group should decide, by consensus or majority vote, its goals, its structure, and the norms of behavior for participants. For example, your group may decide to meet once a month, with the host for that evening being responsible for bringing the munchies. Or your group may commit to providing written feedback for every submission. By establishing these things collaboratively, every member will feel more vested in a successful outcome. Plus, it makes it a lot easier for the leader, or any member of the group, to nail someone nicely if he doesn't follow the established protocol—"Oh, Curtis, when can I expect your written comments about my story?"

Which brings us to the question, Who should be in charge of your group? The answer isn't always obvious because, unlike a class or a workshop where participants pay for a teacher or senior writer's expertise, a critique group is made up of peers. You all serve as teachers and learners, and the last thing you want to do is to distinguish the leader as the *best* writer in the bunch, or the best anything for that matter. It is bad enough when writers are ranked in MFA programs and pitted against each other like gladiators, but it is the kiss of death in a critique group. Yes, I know there are some writers who thrive on competition. An editor once told me about a now-famous mystery writer who confided to her that his writing group fueled him on because he realized he was so much more talented than all the other members. Unlike this fellow, though, most of us do better in groups that foster a sense of community rather than competition.

So if a good writing group functions as a community, then the leader can be thought of as heading up the Neighborhood Watch. While every member contributes to the group's safe, nurturing learning environment, it is the leader's responsibility to keep a watchful eye on the whole. This is a particularly important duty during the story discussions, where most of the crimes are committed. You may want to assign the moderator role to one of the more assertive members of the group, the person naturally gifted at saying things like, "Hey! Excuse me! You two in the corner passing notes, can you please get back to the scene on page 14?"

On the other hand, you may want to rotate leadership, which encourages every member to become more attuned to what constitutes a good (or bad) story discussion. After all, moderating a group discussion isn't rocket science, it is about *paying attention,* a skill every writer should be cultivating anyway.

Who's in Charge?

Let's say you are the group leader for the evening. With you at the meeting, as always, is a room full of separate agendas, biases, needs, insecurities, egos, and personalities. Because of this, many things are likely to require your attention. Here is just one possibility: During the discussion one member disses the story on the table with such authority and vehemence that his negativity sucks in the other group members. As a result, this first negative comment is followed by another, then another, then another, until, before you know it, what you have on your hands is a full-blown *discussion vortex,* a whirling mass of negativity spiraling out of control.

Discussion vortexes happen all the time in groups (and not just writing groups). People's own insecurities and free-floating energy make them susceptible to being swept away by other people's convictions, which is how negativity begets negativity and how an otherwise civilized group of individuals can work itself up into a collective frenzy. As the moderator, this is where you step in. If you sense a discussion vortex gathering momentum, rechannel the energy. Direct the group's attention to a positive aspect of the story. With a single, sincere, positive comment, you can dispel the gathering dark force.

One additional point about discussion vortexes. Groups also can fall into *positive* discussion vortexes, where one paean starts a swirl of hyperbole, until, by the end of the thirty-minute discussion, members are carrying the writer around the room on their shoulders, chanting his name. This is fine, great in fact, if the story is flawless. But if not, you will want to encourage the group to put forth some constructive criticism.

Positive or negative discussion vortexes, or any kind of groupthink in which members conform their opinions to what they believe to be the consensus of the group, eat up a lot of time and energy and can seriously mislead the writer.

Clearly, a big part of your job as moderator is to pay attention to *what* is being said during the story discussion. But you also need to pay attention to *who* is doing the talking. A writing group is not *Jeopardy,* where only the fastest people on the buzzer earn the right to speak. Some group members are good at jumping into the conversation, while others are not. If you are paying attention, you can see these more reserved members leaning forward in their chairs, hands half raised, wishing they would be called on. So call on them. Create a space in the discussion in which they can comfortably insert themselves. "Banana Bread Lady, did you want to say something? We'd love to hear your opinion."

As group leader, you must never grow lax about fostering inclusion. I remember when I was still teaching out of my home, I enjoyed such a familiarity with most of the members that I didn't even bother to vacuum anymore before they came over. One session, a new member joined our group. This new person had just moved to Vermont from Indiana. She brought her knitting to our meetings. For the first few sessions she hardly spoke a word, and, even though I should have been more mindful, I barely registered her participation, other than the fleeting thought that she might be a bit slow. Then one meeting, this newcomer took me aside and quietly asked if I ever organized the discussion by going around the room? She thought it might be a more inviting format for some of the more reserved members of the group, including herself.

Go around the room? What was she talking about? Was that how they did it in Indiana? And who were these other quiet members she was referring to? Our group wasn't quiet. If anything, we were raucous. Exuberant! One big, happy family! My first response to her suggestion was to react defensively, at least in my head. What's more, I don't like going around the room; it makes me feel antsy. I much prefer the spontaneity of "popcorn" discussions, where people can just burst into the conversation at will. I come from a big, loud family with Romanian bloodlines. We've never waited for anyone to finish a sentence in our lives.

Then I remembered that our group was a democracy, and that it wasn't all about me and my preferences. I also recalled that, before I had gotten lazy about my role as moderator, I used to intersperse rounds into the discussion on a regular basis. Rounds are indeed a great way to make sure every voice in the group is heard. They also alleviate the noise and chaos of a free-form discussion, replacing it with a different kind of energy. Rounds raise the anxiety of the group, but in a good way: every member knows they are going to be called on to speak. With rounds, there is no place for slackers to hide, and they know it, so readers take extra care to be prepared.

And so, I launched the next story discussion by suggesting we go around the room to present our feedback. As I awaited my own turn to speak, I realized that we actually had not heard from some of the quieter members of the group for quite a while. It also occurred to me that certain other group members (who shall remain nameless) had been dominating the discussion a bit too much with their loud-mouthed, Romanian ways. And when the group's newest member, the one from Indiana, offered her insights, I could see that she wasn't slow at all. In fact, she was really quite smart, and not just because she could knit and provide feedback at the same time.

I could make a list pages long of all the things that could go wrong in a discussion and that merit the moderator's attention. Groups are so easily sidetracked. We launch the meeting with characters and plot points, but somehow we end up talking about those evil politicians who want to drill for oil in the Arctic or the stain-removing power of the Magic Eraser. We repeat ourselves endlessly and get lost in minutiae—"On page 572, the comma should go inside the quotation marks. Oh, the plot? Yes, whatever, but that comma on page 572 . . ." We get defensive and monopolize the conversation and ask improper questions—"Was your father really a serial killer like the one in the story?" We mismanage the time, we let the energy level drop, and we say mean things about the writer behind her back, even though she is right there in the room with us. We try our best, but we need a leader because somebody, anybody—and that includes you and the Banana Bread Lady—has to be paying attention to all of this stuff. Otherwise, things can get pretty awkward at the grocery store.

Twelve Tips for Moderating a Group Discussion

The key to moderating a discussion effectively is to be restrained, but to always remain in control. Here are some suggestions and convenient phrases you can use to assert your authority gently and keep the discussion running smoothly.

1. **If the discussion is swayed too much toward the negative or positive:** Invite comments that change the trajectory and bring in a fuller perspective. "What was the strongest part of the work and why?" Or, "Does anyone see any missed opportunities or room for wordsmithing?"
2. **If people are talking over each other:** Raise your voice (in a friendly way) and announce, "One person at a time, please."
3. **If the discussion is lackluster:** Ask the writer to read aloud a favorite passage. Ask participants to read aloud their favorite passages as well.
4. **If the writer is being defensive:** Suggest they simply make a note of the issue on their page and revisit it later. "It's just food for thought," is a phrase I often use to stop writers from spending too much time defending or justifying their work.
5. **If the writer isn't hearing the positive:** Make a point to pause the conversation. Ask the writer directly, "Did you hear what that person just said? Did you hear how she called your piece 'exquisite'?"
6. **If the writer's lip is quivering:** That's a sign of feedback overload. End

the conversation and end it with a sincere positive comment about a strength of the work. Also, suggest to the writer the *one* thing (from all the feedback thrown at them) they might want to focus on to move the draft forward.

7. **If someone launches into a feedback filibuster:** Interrupt with, "Hold that thought. Let's hear how the other members feel about some of the issues you've raised."

8. **If one or two members are hogging the discussion:** Switch it up by going around the room so that all the participants can make their points and be heard. You also can direct questions at some of the quieter members of the group as a way to include them in the discussion.

9. **If someone says, "I don't feel I have the right to comment on the story because I'm just a beginner":** Remind them that this is why they're in the room. Any honest response to a work-in-progress is useful to the writer.

10. **If the discussion gets off topic:** One handy comment to reroute the story discussion is, "But we digress. Let's save that conversation for the coffee break." And if members are rehashing the same point, another handy comment is, "Moving on . . ."

11. **If a writer complains to you privately about another participant:** Resist the temptation to gossip. Don't take sides. Advise the person to speak directly to the other participant. Your role is moderator, not mediator.

12. **If someone says something downright mean:** Say something nice and mean it.

MATTHEW SALESSES:
"MAYBE YOU SHOULDN'T BE HERE."

When I asked best-selling author Matthew Salesses, "What's the shittiest feedback you've ever gotten?" he didn't hesitate. A professor in his MFA program once told him, "If you're going to do this kind of writing, maybe you shouldn't be here."

Of course this begged my follow-up question, "What kind of writing were you doing?"

"I was just young and trying out as many things as I could," Matthew explained. "I think that's pretty common, especially for writers at the early stages of their career. But the professor took it as, I was trying to write experimental work and this was a non-experimental place." (Matthew went on to share that this experience was mild compared to what a classmate suffered when a professor tossed that student's manuscript in the trash during his thesis defense.)

Despite initially being nudged toward the door, Matthew did remain in the program and managed to forge connections with other professors and students, some of whom he still exchanges work with twenty years later. He also told me that one of the best pieces of advice he ever received came from his MFA advisor, the novelist Margot Livesey, whom he would show revision after revision. She told him that if he found himself skipping parts while re-reading, it wasn't because those parts were fine, it was because they were probably boring. "That really blew my mind," Matthew said. "I had thought I was skipping those parts because they were perfect, but really I just didn't want to read them. They *were* boring."

Since earning his MFA, as well as a PhD in Literature and Creative

Writing, Matthew has gone on to be both prolific and "essential" (*Buzzfeed* named him one of thirty-two Essential Asian American Writers). From his debut novel *The Hundred-Year Flood* to his latest release, *Disappear Doppelgänger Disappear,* Matthew continues to experiment, commingling surrealism and realism, along with humor and hard truths about Asian stereotypes, white supremacy, and other prevailing social issues.

In addition to being a novelist and essayist, Matthew also serves on the faculty of the MFA/PhD program at Oklahoma State University, and he writes extensively about the art of fiction and pedagogy. His eye-opening book *Craft in the Real World: Rethinking Fiction Writing and Workshopping* challenges traditional Western notions of how we practice and teach craft that propagate "universal" lessons rooted in white, male cultural values that exclude or marginalize writers with diverse backgrounds.

In the following Q&A, Matthew elaborates on how not just craft, but feedback in the real world, could benefit from some serious rethinking to better serve every writer, regardless of race, culture, gender, or a penchant for literary experimentation.

What's the first step to creating a workshop that serves diverse writers?

It depends on what the workshop looks like, the rules of the workshop, and how much it allows for getting to know the author beforehand—their likes and dislikes, and the tradition or context of their work. The more we can learn about that writer's process, the better our perspective to offer useful feedback.

What are some of the most helpful questions to ask writers before giving feedback?

What are you trying to do with your story? Who do you think is your audience? How are you trying to reach your intended audience? What kinds of other stories are you in conversation with? Do you feel like your work is in a certain genre, or are you purposefully mixing genres? Are you writing in a certain literary tradition or experimenting against certain literary traditions? In workshops in America where, say, 70 percent of the participants are probably writing within one [Western] tradition, that majority is on more equal footing when it comes to feedback, even without being given any context. But that's not the case for the other 30 percent.

What are the craft expectations of the traditional Western model that don't necessarily align with other narrative traditions?

The archetypes of Western story structure go back to Aristotle and his ideas about who should be driving the action, meaning an individual hero with agency to make decisions. Who that character is and how he learns—or fails to learn—to be a better citizen through the consequences of his decisions is key to the Western model for story structure, with its need for conflict and for the main character to experience a change. But those aren't necessarily standardized norms of craft in other countries or cultures. In a different tradition, it may be normal for a story to not include conflict, and the hero does not need to have an epiphany. So if we only read or critique through a Western perspective, then those other works will seem like exceptions or experiments, when really they align with a different audience's norms and expectations.

As an Asian American do you think you're a good feedback provider for, say, me, a white woman in Vermont?

I think so. It's probably easier for people in marginalized positions to make the shift to thinking about dominant audiences, because we have a lot of experience reading within the dominant tradition and trying to project ourselves into that dominant audience. It's like what people often say about why people of color are able to write white characters pretty easily, because they're always thinking about white people and how white people see things. Usually, it's more difficult the other way around because people within the majority may not have read much outside that dominant tradition, at least if they didn't have to.

In Craft in the Real World, you presented several models of creative writing workshops. Do you have a favorite?

My favorite is a workshop that allows everybody's stories to be discussed at the same time. It's hard to do because of time constraints, but that's the most fun model and the most like a conversation.

How does that model work?

We usually start talking about a certain question, like how is plot used in these various different texts? Or we might talk about what makes a good ending, and then consider what makes a good ending for each project. Often, this leads to people saying things like, "Okay, here's what I tried to do, but you're doing something different that seems interesting." This gets all of us looking at endings in totally different ways. One of the great things about any workshop is that we learn from other people's processes, but this model foregrounds that benefit. We can have the same type of conversation about one person's work at a time, but the connections then have to be made in the silence between classes, whereas in this model the connections from one story to another start being made right in class.

Assuming we are all educable, is it fair to say everyone can learn how to give useful feedback to a diversity of writers?

I think that's true. Part of it is just the feedback provider acknowledging, "I don't really understand your work from the right perspective, but here is my reaction from my perspective." With that, writers then know this feedback might be coming from outside their audience, so they have context to understand how to take the comment.

DON'T TAKE THIS PERSONALLY

You know when someone starts a sentence by saying, "Don't take this personally," it almost always means they're about to say something you don't want to hear. And then of course you are even more likely to take whatever they have to say personally, if only because they told you not to. Ah, human nature.

In a workshop or one-to-one feedback exchange, the challenge of not taking criticism personally is an ongoing practice. It's hard not to feel a prickle, for example, when someone pronounces, "I think your novel's heroine is shallow and uninteresting!" when, in fact, you based said heroine on yourself. In situations like these, it takes an evolved human being to resist a retort like, "Well, I think *you're* shallow and uninteresting."

As much as that type of response feels great on a playground, a more useful course of action is to hear the feedback not as a censure of your personality but as insight into characterization. In light of this feedback (admittedly a bit ham-handed), you might want to revisit your main character to look for missed opportunities where you might give her more depth or nuance. This is not to suggest you should fundamentally reinvent your heroine (shallow-seeming characters can be wickedly engaging), but instead consider how you might round her out on the page. Hint at a hidden complexity. Suggest a depth of character.

To do so, you always have at your disposal one or all of those handy narrative techniques—action, detail, dialogue, and internal monologue—that allow you to "show" your narrator or protagonist more fully, inside and out. You may also consider infusing the narrative with more backstory at opportune moments to give your main character multidimensionality, even if she spends much of her time in the present tense of the narrative (aka plot) considering cheek implants. (Which, to my point, does not connote shallowness, unless, from a reader's perspective, that is all she seems to do or think about on the page, with no hint of why.)

For fiction writers, the challenges of not taking criticism personally can be met by a sharp metaphoric slap to the forehead. *Oh, wait, I'm not being critiqued, my writing is. How can I translate the commentary into craft?*

But what about writers of narrative nonfiction? Criticism in this realm may be even harder to depersonalize, given you—or at least some iteration of you—are the "me" in the memoir; you are the person in the personal essay. It is your life experience, as you perceived it, rendered on the page. Thus, when readers question, for example, the behavior of the narrator, it can feel like you personally are being judged. Similarly, if readers say something like, "I can't believe anyone would do such a thing," it feels like your integrity is being put into question. No wonder when we hear negative responses to our true stories our first impulse is often defensive.

"But that's how it really happened!"

"You don't understand. I had to stay in the marriage for the sake of my children."

"How dare you criticize me when you weren't even there."

One of the things that can make it even more difficult to hear feedback on our personal stories is the binary language feedback providers often use when they critique the work. We tend to talk in terms of "liking" or "not liking" the people in a story, which of course is how we frequently talk about people in real life. For example, more than my family would ever like to hear, I have said I don't like my ex-neighbor with whom I used to share a driveway. The woman started more than one conversation with me with the sentence, "I'd hate to get my lawyer involved." Plus, she had a habit of putting her recycling out a day early, which just screamed control freak, and I often caught her peering into the messy backseat of my Toyota, probably hoping to find contraband. I just don't like her (there, I said it again!), and whether that is my problem or hers, I don't care.

But in a manuscript, even a nonfiction one, there are no people to like or dislike. There are only characters, either well-characterized or in need of further characterization. Even you—the narrator of your personal narrative—is not really you, but rather a persona, a performative "I." In essence, the you in your memoir is a projection of yourself made manifest by what you choose to share or not share in the text. I would go so far as to say that the "I" in a memoir is no different from the narrator in a work of fiction, in respect to how important it is to craft your way onto the page, using those same scenic/showing techniques I mentioned a few paragraphs prior (action, significant detail, dialogue, internal monologue). Those are the narrative techniques, when selectively chosen and seamlessly integrated, that allow your real and nonreal characters to feel authentic and come alive on the page. The only (big) difference, of course, is that in nonfiction you can't make stuff up, not about yourself or anyone else in your story.

There is probably no way during a manuscript discussion to stop feedback providers from talking about characters in terms of liking or not liking them. Believe me, I have tried, plus I am often the worst culprit. On the other hand, there are worse ways to respond to a manuscript, like indifference. At least when readers express strong emotions about the people on your pages it shows they are emotionally invested, even if they end up siding with the character you intended to be unsympathetic.

More to the point, whom your readers like and dislike may be informative, but swaying their affinities isn't your main objective. Why? Because your job isn't to get readers to like "you" (the narrator of your story), or to agree with your actions, or to loathe your ex-husband or even your litigious neighbor. Indeed, just having that agenda often leads to heavy-handed characterization, an overkill of forcing your judgments on us, which is likely to backfire. Rather, your job is to create *credible* characters, characters we believe in and understand, characters we really get to know. And, paradoxically, the more we know about a character—specifically the narrator—the more we are inclined to like the you in your story, or at least feel sympathy or empathy for that you, even when you expose your flaws; in fact, especially when you expose your flaws. This is the type of narrator we can relate to, if not in the particulars, then in our shared humanness. We all screw up, but only the most courageous writers among us are willing to put our mistakes and vulnerabilities out there on the page.

The truth is, even when all is said and rewritten, no writer can fully control how their characters are perceived, neither in the drafting stage nor after the book is released. Readers are going to form judgments, some you may never have intended, some that surprise the heck out of you. With that in mind, imagine the lady in your online writing group who offered this bit of feedback, "I just don't understand why you stayed in the marriage." Perhaps your first impulse remains defensive. *Of course she wouldn't understand,* you think, *the woman lives in Malibu. She probably goes through husbands the same way she downs skinny cocktails.*

I can't judge you too harshly for such a reaction because that sounds exactly like what I would be thinking, and I even have good friends in Malibu! But for both our sakes, let me advise here that you might want to follow that first impulse with a more thoughtful reaction, one that better serves you and your writing. Let Ms. Malibu's comment inspire you to revisit your characterization with fresh eyes, informed by the subtext of her feedback. Is there more you can do to allow readers to fully share in your narrator's perspective? Have you overlooked opportunities to both show and tell more clearly her (and by "her" I mean "your") marital relationship, motivation, and circumstances?

It always bums me out when otherwise motivated people remain on the threshold of writing personal narratives for fear of exposing themselves or others in their story and being judged. This feels like such a waste, because few things are more worthwhile than capturing on the page the events of your life, whether extraordinary, uplifting, tragic, entertaining, or quietly significant. What a way to grow! What a way to serve readers by broadening our perspectives, engendering our empathy, and reinforcing our collective humanity.

Yet here is another reality for memoirists and other tellers of true stories—one that can feel as daunting as our fear of exposure: Yes, we all have stories worthy of sharing with the world, but the onus is on us to capture those life experiences on the page in a way that makes them mean as much to outsiders as they do to us. No different than fiction writers, authors of narrative nonfiction must mingle craft and art to immerse readers in a point of view (meaning our own perspective), enabling others to see what we see, know what we know, feel what we feel. Thankfully, we have feedback providers to help us confront these narrative challenges, draft by draft by draft.

As someone who loves to write personal essays, I will always remember what a teacher in graduate school said to me after I submitted a piece about a deeply meaningful experience. The event was a watershed moment in my life. All my editorial instincts knew that this situation made for a powerful story. How could readers not see how I had weathered the storm and took from it a powerful life lesson? How could such a traumatic tale not have the same impact on others as it did on me?

"You don't get credit for living," my teacher said, handing the draft back to me for another revision. "You have to make it play on the page."

Distinguishing the "Writer" from the "Narrator"

Earlier in this chapter, I noted that it is important to distinguish the narrator in a personal story from the actual writer of the story. Yes, the former is a persona of the latter, but the writing process is served by thinking of your narrator not as you but as a character separate from you. During story discussions, feedback providers can help reinforce this concept (and skirt the appearance of judging the writer herself) by referring to the "I" in the work as "the narrator," rather than conflating that I with the writer. Below is an example of what I mean.

Not-so-good feedback provider (turning to the writer whose memoir is being discussed): "Why the hell would *you* steal a car!?"

Good feedback provider: "It would better help me understand why *your narrator* stole the car if you offered a bit more direct thought or backstory."

THE TOP TEN RULES OF A SUCCESSFUL WRITING GROUP

W. Somerset Maugham reportedly once said, "There are three rules for writing the novel. Unfortunately no one knows what they are." I'd like to add here that there are also rules for writing groups . . . and I think I've figured them out.

We come together in a workshop or critique group to do important work, but little things can get in the way, like misconceptions about what to expect or what is expected of us. That is why successful writing groups establish parameters up front, from how frequently participants can submit their work to how many pages for each submission. Successful groups also abide by a set of rules—a code of conduct, if you will—that helps keep everybody honest and raises the quality of the discussion. Below are my personal top ten rules of a successful workshop. You can bend them, but don't break them, and I promise your group will thrive.

1. **Make a point to show up.** Absenteeism is demoralizing to the writer whose work is being discussed, and it undermines the energy and collective commitment of the group. Plus, if you don't show up, how can you learn from the story discussions?

2. **Be prepared.** Read the manuscripts and prepare your critiques *before* the meeting. Otherwise you will be playing catch-up in class, reading when you should be listening or scribbling down comments when you should be contributing to the discussion.

3. **No whining about the in-class writing exercises.** It doesn't matter if they make you nervous or you think they are dumb; do them anyway. It is only ten or fifteen minutes of your time, and one of these days you are

bound to get something out of them, like maybe a plot breakthrough or the start of a great story.

4. **Don't submit anything that is non-negotiable.** If you have no intention of changing a word of your manuscript, then perhaps you would be better served by a copy of *Writer's Market* than a writing group.

5. **No bystanders allowed.** It is important that every group member submits something for critique on a regular basis. If you don't, it is too easy to sit in judgment when critiquing other writers' efforts. Plus, you are missing the heart of the experience.

6. **Put yourself in the writer's place.** When providing feedback, your best guide is to remember what it feels like to have your own work critiqued.

7. **Avoid comparisons.** Maybe the novelist next to you can't write like Tolstoy, but then again Dostoevsky couldn't write like Tolstoy. Comparisons within the group only get in the way of helping writers develop their own voices.

8. **Separate the writing from the writer.** Whether working in fiction or narrative nonfiction, writers are more likely to be guarded if the other members of the group have a habit of asking intrusive questions like, "Was that really true?" "Did that really happen?" "I can't stand the way your mother treated you." Accept and discuss each work as a piece of writing, not personal history.

9. **Don't plagiarize.** No matter how much you love someone else's plotline or concept or language, don't lift it for your next work. And especially don't lift it and then present it to the group for critique.

10. **Respect each other's privacy.** Don't show a writer's submission to anyone outside of the group, unless that person has given you permission.

CRYSTAL WILKINSON: "PROCESSING FEEDBACK HAS TO BE A MEDITATION."

In the good old days, before Crystal Wilkinson had published her first short-story collection, *Blackberries, Blackberries,* named Best Debut Fiction by *Today's Librarian* magazine, she could take creative-writing classes and work-shops anytime she wanted. Now, as a much-celebrated author and an associate professor of English in the MFA in Creative Writing Program at the University of Kentucky, it's not so easy.

"I love being in workshops and being a student," Crystal said, "but if I try to take a class with one of my friends teaching it, they feel I'm infring-ing because they know I'm published; it's not a true student kind of thing. I miss not having more feedback," she adds. "That's how I thrived and got my first two books written." Crystal's writing career has gone on to include three prize-winning works of fiction, plus *Perfect Black,* a memoir in verse. She also serves as Poet Laureate of Kentucky and is the recipient of a 2021 O. Henry Prize, as well as numerous other awards and fellowships.

Crystal, who grew up in Southern Appalachia and describes herself as "country," recalls working on her first novel under contract. "This sounds crazy," she says, but the pressure made her miss "five million deadlines." Her agent would check in and say, "How's it going?" and Crystal would say, "Yep, I'm still going." At the time, the experience made her think that, for the next book, she'd rather write it without a contract up front. "I can't write at my best when I feel the breath on my neck," she explains. "Something about being published ruins everything," she laughs.

An author who claims "an affinity for the blank page," she has found the process of writing a novel—of always having to move forward—unsettling.

"Writing has always been easy for me," Crystal says, "but having your head around a novel, staying committed to this larger thing, the density of the work and all the situations, it's like holding up a world. Being in the middle of it is still play," she adds, "but getting to it is daunting. Every time I pull it up on the screen, I think, *Ugh, there you all are, ready to get on my nerves.*"

For help along the way, Crystal has relied on a few steady friends, including Nikky Finney, a writer and teacher whom she met years ago through the Affrilachian Poets, a Kentucky-based writing group whose members identify as both African American and Appalachian. Given the women's busy schedules and the fact that they lived three hours apart, the situation required some improvising. For a while, the two met Sunday afternoons to read aloud new work and swap verbal feedback. (Neither had the time nor energy to critique one more written manuscript.) They also checked in and motivated each other in other ways. Crystal describes a phone call from Nikky—"Okay, Crissy, get up. It's 4:00 a.m. Put some water on your face. Here we go."

When asked about how she processes feedback, Crystal explains, "I don't take suggestions literally. I go in and try to figure out, why is it unclear? Is there a missed opportunity here where this needs to be opened up? Do I need to get rid of it all? Do I need a bulldozer or a brushstroke?" Crystal's method is to revise surrounded by pages marked up with other people's comments. "Feedback takes me someplace different altogether," she says. "It makes me really think about the work."

As a teacher, Crystal recognizes the danger of workshops if students don't process feedback appropriately. She describes an "amazing" writer in one of her classes who took every suggestion from the other students and went down the list, revising her story. "She ruined it. Totally ruined it," Crystal says. "As writers, we're looking for that validation and approval of others, so we get caught in thinking, *If I do all these fixes, everyone will like it.* You have to practice that ability to stand back and do a meditation on the whole piece."

From her own graduate student days at Spalding University, Crystal recalls workshopping one of her stories that later appeared in her short story collection *Water Street.* "I was one of those rare birds in grad school that already had a book contract, so I had that breath-on-my-neck thing going already and was anxious to get feedback." The piece, entitled "My Girl Mona," was about a woman talking to her psychiatrist about her memories of a childhood friend who turned out to not be a good friend at all. Early in the discussion, a few readers, including the professor, decided that the story was about a woman with a split personality. This had never been Crystal's intent. "During the feedback, you're not supposed to talk," Crystal says, "so I kept silent, trying to be the good girl, but what I should have done is stopped them because once the professor got on board with that idea, all the students followed suit. All the feedback was about the 'Sybil' factor, and I got nothing out of it."

When Crystal senses this kind of snowball effect building among her own students, she tries to stop it by inviting dissenting opinions. A similar danger occurs when students "preworkshop" a story, arriving at class with a collective opinion. Recalling her own story, "My Girl Mona," which became one of the pivotal pieces in her linked collection, she worried right through the galley stage of her book that the story didn't work; that maybe she should have "fixed" the main character whom the class had assigned a split personality. Her worries were unfounded. "My Girl Mona" won the *Indiana Review* Fiction Prize, and the collection was a finalist for both the Orange Prize and a Zora Neal Hurston / Richard Wright Foundation Legacy Award in fiction. The main character in "My Girl Mona" also seeded her first novel, *The Birds of Opulence.*

"Processing feedback has to be a meditation," Crystal reiterates. "Otherwise, you'll slaughter your story."

MEET THE WORLD'S
WORST WORKSHOP

Any workshop instructor can tell you there are certain types of participants who show up in their classes on a regular basis and irritate the bejesus out of everybody else. It is easy to recognize these types when they are sitting next to you, ruining the group dynamic, but it isn't so easy to recognize when you are one of them. For example, when I was working on this chapter, I asked other writing teachers what types of participants they would include in the world's worst workshop. My list overlapped with theirs with one exception—the Nervous Talker. Eventually, I figured out why this personality type had never occurred to me. *I* am the Nervous Talker. I am that participant who fills in every quiet interlude with my own white noise. Once I start talking, I can't seem to shut myself up.

We all have aspects of our personality that could use some work.

What follows is a class roster for the world's worst workshop. If you recognize yourself in any of these types, take credit for being honest. Then take a few moments to think about how you might modify your behavior the next time you engage in a writing discussion (or in a business meeting, or at a dinner party, or in the quiet car on the train). Meanwhile, I'll just be sitting here not saying a word, giving you a chance to read in peace, though you might catch me wringing my hands if the silence goes on for too long.

The Shadow: You show up at every meeting, but you never volunteer any comments. What if you said something wrong! Unlike some members of the group who could use some lessons in manners (oh yes, you have your opinions, you're just not wont to air them in public), you never exhibit bad behavior or annoy the other workshop participants, mostly because they've forgotten you exist.

The Star: It's remarkable how you always manage to be the first person in the group to have your work discussed. Yes, some of the members have dissenting opinions about your gifts, but those people didn't have an essay published in *Chicken Soup for the (Golfer's) Soul.* Besides, you're only here to see if the instructor wants to schedule a round at the country club so he can introduce you to his agent. Sometimes you feel guilty that you never bother to read anyone else's submissions, but writers have to be selfish. Faulkner didn't even attend his own son's birthday party.

The Grammarian: Of course you'd love to join in all the fun talking about a story's themes or the feelings a poem evokes, but someone has to put first things first. If you don't drive home the fact that a participial phrase at the beginning of a sentence must refer to the grammatical subject, then who else is going to do it? You're well aware of what others whisper behind your back—"obsessive," "nitpicky," "weirdo"—but they'll never find fault with your punctuation. If you've told the group once, you've told them a thousand times, "Using an exclamation point is like laughing at your own jokes!"

The Devil's Advocate: If someone says black, you say white; not because you give a crap about white, but because it's fun to stir up trouble. After all, isn't that what your old man did whenever he made it to the supper table? "Dad, my soup is cold." "Like hell it is." "Dad, I want to be a writer." "Like hell you do." That's what you call character building. That's how you learned to be a man, and fend for yourself after your dad got sent to the big house. A social worker once described you as oppositional. Like hell you are. Anyway, writing isn't for sissies.

The Interrupter: You're impulsive and, yes, you'll admit it, patience isn't your strong suit. Other people start talking and you just have to run with their ideas, or cut them off if they're saying something stupid. Some people call you rude. Then again some people take forever to say what they have to say. Besides, the other group members are just as bad, always interrupting you to ask, "Will you *please* let me finish?" Then half the time when you do let them finish, they can't even remember what they were going to say. Now what does that tell you?

The Outpatient: You figure a writing group is cheaper than therapy so you come to the meetings to work through your issues and connect with other emerging souls. You know your weeping is a distraction, but in that last story, the way the husband took out the trash, it just brought it all back—how you and your last lover shared so many domestic routines during the two months you were together. He left without taking the self-portrait you wove him for his birthday. He left without providing a forwarding address. Oh, it's so healing, to share those feelings.

The Social Conscience: Your hybrid car is smothered in bumper stickers. You once spent a night in jail for verbally assaulting a smoker. *Everything* you write is a political act. Wake up, people! If you've told the writers in your group once, you've told them ad nauseum, we all have a moral imperative to preach truth to power, to save the world. The rainforest is being destroyed at a rate of 2.4 acres per second. Now that's conflict! Third World countries are struggling under a $523 billion debt burden. Now that's crisis! And in the United States alone, per-capita meat consumption has risen dramatically in the past twenty years. Now that's just gross!

The Bibliophile: From the ancient classics to the must-reads of the twenty-first century, you've read them all, and doesn't everybody know it. You've got a recommended reading list to accompany every submission. "Have you read the *Iliad?* Now that's how you do battle scenes!" "Be sure to check out Margaret Atwood. Her speculative fiction addresses your themes of gender and identity brilliantly." You also make a point to keep everybody current, like when you let one of the other workshop participants know that the best-selling author Sally Rooney had just come out with a brilliant new book with a plot identical to hers, so maybe they ought to reconsider.

The Voice of Experience: What a lucky coincidence—the writer's main character is a competitive kickboxer, and so are you. And that poem you discussed last week about whooping cranes—you know all about whooping cranes, thanks to an uncle who used to rehabilitate them. Oh, and in that story where the narrator drives an RV cross-country— you once drove an RV from St. Louis to Seattle, but never again. No way! In fact, it's hard to believe any character would drive all that way when flying is so much faster. One thing you know for certain, if something in another writer's story doesn't mirror your personal experience, then readers are not going to believe it.

The Rewriter: You just wish the others in your monthly poetry group would share their pages for critique in a more punctual manner. That way you'd have more time to rewrite all their poems the way they should have been written in the first place. You've always been someone who likes to lead by example, so why leave revision to the amateurs when you can fix their language and punctuation and line breaks for them. You'd think they'd appreciate your remarkable generosity, but instead they've started meeting without you. And this after all that time you spent helping them write just as well as you!

The Lark: You're in the group because you love being around writers (they're so *intense*), and because the swing-dance class you had hoped to take on Thursday evenings was already filled. You can't help it that you're always late to the meetings; it's just the way you are. You usually arrive in the middle of a writing exercise, which is perfect timing since you always bring food and can set up the spread while the others are trying to focus. "Dim sum, anyone?!" It's a shame you haven't had time to get your own story idea down on paper, but you told the members of the group all about it during class, and they thought it was really good!

Those Who Can't Do . . . : It's demoralizing having to teach amateurs who think writing "might be fun." Plus, it's *their* fault you haven't been able to write anything new, not since your debut novel came out over a decade ago ("astonishingly complex," wrote the *Providence Journal;* "a ripening talent" declared the *Denver Post*). You know your comments in class come across as harsh—"Nobody's going to give a damn about your childhood!"; "A nun could write better sex scenes!"—but you're only doing these people a favor. Why feed their hopes? Besides, it hurts when your students go on to get published.

PUBLISHING 101

The last time I went to a panel discussion on how to get published, it took me months to recover.

The representative from one of the big publishing houses spent most of her time talking about the need for aspiring authors to immerse themselves in market research and amass thousands of followers on social media.

The independent publisher was nothing but gloom and doom about the challenges facing small presses.

The hybrid publisher brought me to my knees when she quoted the fee for their services.

The agent warned, "Be prepared to get your heart broken, because publishers are in the business of making money, so the literary merits of a work won't be enough to make it sell."

And the aged and esteemed author on the panel kept bemoaning the fact that editors today don't even edit. "Maxwell Perkins must be rolling over in his grave!"

The panel concluded with a string of dire warnings: "Don't quit your day job." "Don't expect writing to feed your goldfish, let alone your family." "Don't think getting published will make you happy." (That last comment being obvious, from the scowl on the esteemed author's face.)

Now, with several of my own books in print, I can understand why insiders feel the need to give aspiring authors a reality check about the business of publishing. Like the doom-and-gloom panelists, I also find myself feeling compelled to warn the uninitiated about the challenges that lie ahead. The other day a woman told me that she had a great idea for a book about her now-healthy seven-year-old son. The mother's emotions were palpable as she described the boy's struggle to overcome a rare disease, and how he had defied his doctor's bleak prediction that he wouldn't survive past infancy. Meanwhile, the whole time this woman was talking I was thinking, *Yeah, yeah, everybody's got a great book idea. So what makes your kid's story any better than all the rest?*

That's when I knew it was time for another reality check. Not the kind you get from publishing panels and insiders, but the kind you can only get from being around people who are engaged in the act of writing. Aspiring authors benefit from the company of other writers for all sorts of reasons, one of the most important being to serve as a reminder that our work matters outside the publishing realm, separate from its marketing or income-earning potential. With this kind of feedback—an affirmation of the writing process itself—writers learn one of the first and most important lessons about publishing. If you write what truly interests you, if you write from the heart, you are more likely to produce the kind of books that publishers will ultimately buy.

Yes, finding a publisher can be challenging, and the word most of us are likely to hear a lot is "pass." On the other hand, writers are offered contracts every day—so why not you? Why not me? One of the things I've learned in my own efforts to get published is that it helps to go to panel discussions to understand the business of publishing, but it also helps to be part of a community who know how to mix business with pleasure. Here are ten good reasons why writers should stick together before, during, and after you see your books in print.

Relatability. You know how mothers love to swap childbirth stories, even if their children are now in their fifties? Writers enjoy the same kind of bonding experience when talking about creating their books. "How long did it take?" "Was it painful?" "Did you opt for drugs or go without?" Who else but another writer can fully appreciate the gory details and rewards of this labor of love we call writing?

Perspective. I used to feel sorry for myself because I often have to get up at 4:00 a.m. to find enough quality time to write. Then I kept meeting or reading about other writers who do the exact same thing. Writers get up at 4:00 a.m. That's just what we do, whether you're a working parent or a retired insurance executive like Ted Kooser, the former poet laureate of the United States. Understanding this fact of a writer's life has not only given me perspective, but also the names of people I can call if I need someone to talk to at that ridiculous hour.

Deadlines. Some of the most prolific members of my workshop can't seem to write between sessions. This actually works to my advantage, since most of these writers have advanced well beyond my teaching abilities, yet they still need me for my deadlines. Yes, setting a deadline with no real consequences is a bit of a contrivance. (What are you going to do if a workshop participant fails to deliver—fine them?) Nevertheless, it works. Most writers are motivated to produce when they know someone, anyone, is expecting to read their work by a certain time.

Persistence. The writing process has two components. There is the *fun* part when you are captivated with the newness of your idea and the words just flow. And then there is the *Are we having fun, yet?* part when you realize you've got another couple hundred pages to go before you complete a first draft. The echo of encouragement from your last meeting with your writing group can make all the difference when deciding whether to sit down and write for the next three hours or plant some more beans in the garden. That support can also make a difference when the time comes to shop around your manuscript, given many published authors tell tales of having to send twenty, fifty, or even a hundred or more query letters to agents before finally getting representation.

Preparing for your big debut. Why-oh-why do some of the contestants on *American Idol* make their singing debut on national television? Wasn't there anyone who cared enough to tell them to practice a few more years in front of a full-length mirror? As a writer, you don't want to submit your work to a discriminating audience of agents or editors before you've honed your talents. By getting feedback throughout the drafting process, you will improve your work, and your chances for making a good first impression.

Confidence. Related to the previous point, an editor of a literary magazine told me she knows after reading just the first few paragraphs of a submission whether the piece is publishable. "There is an authority in the writing," she explained, "a sense that the writer has reached a point of confidence appropriate for publication." Among the two hundred submissions this editor receives weekly, those that exude confidence on page 1 are the only stories she bothers reading to completion. Other writers can help you test your own authority *before* you submit a piece. Ask them if your opening paragraphs inspire them to keep reading.

Contacts. An acclaimed psychiatrist sent his self-help book to two agents. They both rejected it for the same reason: too academic. So he rewrote it in a voice more appropriate for a general readership, but then he worried that it wasn't any good. A writer/friend finally bullied him into letting her read it, and she loved the new draft so much she insisted on giving it to her agent. Now the psychiatrist is the author of an "entertaining and literate" best seller, underscoring the fact that when you are trying to get published, the right voice is important, but so are pushy writer/friends with contacts in the business.

Illegitimi Non Carborundum ("**Don't Let the Bastards Grind You Down**"). Intellectually, you know when a publisher rejects your work it might not have anything to do with whether it's good or bad. Getting published is as much about fit as quality—hitting up the right publisher at the right time. Understanding this, however, still doesn't stop you from feeling deflated when you get that rejection. One thing that does help, however, is commiserating with other talented writers who are amassing their own paper logs of rejections, some of them even bigger than yours. Indeed, some creative communities have started "rejection collections," which are basically spreadsheets recording everyone's rejections to exemplify how "normal" it is to hear "pass" and to take the shame out of the sting.

Editing. You've got a book deal. Hurray! But as that aged and esteemed author on the publishing panel declared, your developmental editor may not actually do much developmental editing of your work. Indeed, a number of acquiring editors at publishing houses may be focused more on making deals than modifying manuscripts. This is potentially bad news for both you and your reading public. One solution is to hire a book doctor or freelance editor (check references and do a test chapter), but a more affordable alternative is to find a great workshop or qualified critique partner willing to pinch hit as your editor, with the promise, of course, that you will return the favor when her book is accepted by a publisher.

The Book Party. You're a published author! It's time for a celebration. Who better to invite to your book party than all the other writers who helped you along the way by affirming the creative process, providing you with perspective and deadlines, sharing their publishing contacts, commiserating with you when the manuscript was rejected, and lending you their editorial expertise before and after your work was accepted. This is a party commemorating the publication of your book, but it is also a celebration of what can be achieved when writers connect with other writers.

JODI PICOULT:
"I CALL OUR RELATIONSHIP MY
SECOND MARRIAGE."

When Jodi Picoult graduated from Princeton with a degree in English and creative writing, several literary agents came knocking, eager for a look at her thesis/novel. "There weren't a lot of creative-writing programs at the time, so anyone writing a thesis got solicited by the big agencies," Jodi says. "It was exciting, flattering." Among the first to approach her was a woman from mega-agency ICM. A few weeks later, this same woman also earned the distinction of being the first agent to reject Jodi's manuscript. "Something about it not being what she was looking for, standard rejection stuff," Jodi remembers.

In her quest for an agent, Jodi amassed hundreds of rejections, the kind of collective negative feedback that might have deterred a less-determined writer. Jodi persevered, however, and two years after her first rejection, she heard from Laura Gross, an agent just starting out in the business. "Laura loved the book's character development and the voice I seemed to have, apparently even back then," Jodi says. "I think it's rare for a twenty-one-year-old to turn out a well-crafted novel. It bodes well for things to come, and I think Laura saw this."

At that point, Laura hadn't yet sold anything to any publisher, but Jodi trusted her. "I think what I responded to was the way she presented selling my book as something *we* would do together, instead of her doing it *for* me. It made me feel like I had a partner in what would prove to be a long, continuous minefield of publishing, and I never forgot that."

Laura spent a year trying to sell Jodi's Princeton novel, to no avail. ("Thankfully," Jodi admits, "that manuscript will never be published.") Meanwhile, Jodi completed a master's in education at Harvard and worked several jobs, including teaching creative writing to middle and high school students. In 1991, the same year Jodi was pregnant with her first child, she finished a new novel, *Songs of the Humpback Whale.* Laura sold the book to Faber and Faber within three months, and the novel was published the next year. Since those salad days, author and agent have enjoyed a tight friendship and professional partnership for over two decades and twenty-eight internationally best-selling novels (plus a few musicals and television and movie adaptations of her books). "I call our relationship my second marriage," Jodi smiles.

In looking back, Jodi recalls a particularly notable interaction *not* with Laura, which happened shortly after her tenth novel, *Second Glance,* had just made the *New York Times* best-seller list. That same year, Jodi received the New England Bookseller Award for Fiction, recognizing her body of work as a significant contribution to New England's culture. Out of the blue, Jodi's publicist received a call from a high-powered agent at ICM. The woman wanted to fly her to New York City for lunch and talk about representing her work. As Jodi was listening to her publicist relay this news, it hit her. The woman's name . . . ICM . . . this was the same agent who first rejected Jodi's Princeton manuscript. "Everyone wants to back a winner," she laughs.

Even as one of the best-selling authors on the planet, Jodi still feels flattered to be wooed. Nevertheless, she told her publicist to decline the woman's invitation to lunch. She was completely happy with her current agent. "I didn't trust myself to have any contact with her," says Jodi, who doubts if the ICM agent even remembers rejecting her manuscript all those years ago. "It would have been nice to rub it in her face, but I don't live my life like that."

Jodi did tell her agent about the unexpected phone call. The next day, in appreciation for her loyalty, Laura sent Jodi flowers. "But honestly," Jodi adds, "usually I'm the one sending them to her after she's negotiated a particularly good deal!"

CAN CREATIVE WRITING BE TAUGHT?

A creative-writing instructor once informed me, "You know, you can't really teach creative writing. People come to my class, and they're writers or they're not." *Says who?* I thought. And how can you tell the difference—from their GPAs? Their ability to pronounce the word *anathema*? Their third drafts?

I think this instructor has it all wrong (and suffers from a decidedly sad-sack attitude). I think creative writing can be taught, and if it can't then why are thousands of creative-writing teachers at universities and community colleges and MFA programs still on the payroll? For proof creative writing can be taught, just hold up any sincere student's first draft and fourth draft, then drive a truck through the gap in narrative quality.

Still, the issue persists; and with it a lingering whiff of academic elitism—"You are either born a writer, or forget it." I blame this elitism on Thomas Jefferson, a man who promoted education as "the equalizer of all children" but clarified that for the "laboring" class, the basic level of elementary education would suffice. I also blame it on King Charles (or, more likely, that damn Camilla), who once wrote in a memo to a senior-staff member of his household, "What is wrong with everyone nowadays? Why do they all seem to think they are qualified to do things far beyond their technical capabilities?"

What is wrong with everyone, indeed?! Who are all these students who join writing communities with the hope of learning the aspects of creative writing—characterization, plot, setting, point of view, metaphor, prose rhythm, and the like? And even if they can be taught craft, good creative writing requires more than mastery of a certain skill set. It requires inspiration! It is an art! Perhaps one or two "ordinary" students might be struck by the proverbial bolt of lightning, if they are lucky, but we all know that it is much more likely to hit the pale, lanky fellow with the wire rims, two desks over—the "gifted" student, as he is often referred to by the instructors in the faculty lounge.

From first grade on, teachers have tried to tag the writers in their classrooms, but it is never as easy as it seems. "Oh, Darryl, he's the *writer* in the class." Then twelve years later, Darryl goes on to be a NASCAR driver and never writes another word beyond his autograph. The same thing happens in MFA programs. "Shhh! Don't tell anybody, but we've ranked Virginia the least likely student to succeed as a writer. No funding for her, I'm afraid!" Then, after graduation, the low-ranked Virginia manages to defy the program's expectations and write five best-selling novels, allowing her to eventually pay off her enormous student debt.

The funny thing about writers is, you can't always distinguish them from the flunkies or science majors or loggers of the world. At least not right away. For years, a student's talent may remain dormant, but then suddenly (after years of scribbling) she discovers her own voice, or a bit of encouragement, or a fictional technique that finally solves that niggling problem she's been having with transitions—and bloom! The person everyone assumed was "unteachable" emerges as a wonderful writer.

Can creative writing be taught? In the classroom, everything we do is a form of feedback that contributes to the answer to that question, from our attitudes about writing and teaching, to the students we single out for praise and attention, to the unspoken signals we project. Even when we know enough not to say something outright dismissive or negative, it is so easy to inadvertently send a discouraging message. One evening when I was teaching an essay-writing class, I realized something startling. I found myself sitting with my chair turned a certain direction in our circle, my back literally to one of the members of the group; the member who happened to show the least promise.

Yes, creative writing can be taught, but to succeed teachers need to take it on faith that every student that comes to them can learn, from the undergrad who is trying too hard to be Sally Rooney, to the executive who writes so tidily her sentences have hospital corners, to the octogenarian who can't use a computer but wants to preserve the family stories for her grandchildren. There is a reason these participants found their way to those chairs in the circle or squares in your Zoom screen. They must have some affinity for writing or they wouldn't have had the gumption to show up in the first place. As creative-writing teachers, one of the most important parts of our job is to honor *every* student with the distinction of being the writer in the class, because just that feedback alone can make a remarkable difference.

Below are a few tips for teaching creative writing.

Create a nurturing learning environment. By fostering a sense of community rather than competition, students will be more willing to put forth their own voices and story material, not imitative prose that simply reflects the style of a famous author, or the class darling, or whatever type of writing happens to be in vogue in contemporary literary culture.

Push students to write, write, write. The first hurdle to creative writing is intimidation. The second is procrastination. The only way to help students overcome both is to immerse them in the writing process. Doing is the fastest route to learning.

Give them a prompt. Some students aren't sure what to write about or where to start. That's where writing exercises and short assignments come in handy, helping students overcome the intimidation of the blank page and connect to the ideas and stories that are percolating just beneath their consciousness.

Encourage the play. A lot of students who have the ability to write, can't, because they have internal naysayers nagging them all the time. "What would your mother think?" "Who do you think you are, using all those fancy-pants words!" "That's a horrible sentence. And why don't you write something people want to read?" The best thing we can do for our students is to help them silence those voices and just go for it during the outpouring stage (aka the "down draft" or the "rehearsal draft"). There should be no shaming of early efforts because the first draft is the only draft where it is all good, because discovery, not craft, is what matters.

Build up their skills. Urge students to let their protagonists act, not just be acted upon. Encourage them to use active verbs to energize the language, and not to confuse dialogue with conversation. The more tricks of the trade you share about craft through mini-lessons, in-depth discussions, constructive criticism, and sincere praise, the more you empower your students.

Bring literature down to earth. Creative-writing students need to learn to read as writers, not as English majors. To that end, it helps to analyze Hemingway's signature terse prose, or his use of objective correlatives, rather than his literary themes. It also helps to mention that the author rewrote the ending of *A Farewell to Arms* thirty-nine times.

Don't just referee story discussions, set the lead. If you take the writer and his work seriously, if you provide specific constructive feedback, and if you make a point to keep the discussion upbeat, then students will model your behavior when critiquing each other's work. What you don't want them to model, however, are all your opinions, so be sure to invite different points of view, and don't always offer your feedback first.

Reiterate key points. In a lively story discussion the comments come fast and furious, and not every feedback provider is perfectly articulate. Help the group process all the information by making a point to reiterate, translate, elaborate, summarize, or adjudicate throughout the discussion.

Personalize the process. Insecure students benefit from relentless encouragement and gentle guidance; other students may be able to handle bigger doses of constructive criticism; and all students improve when you show them you believe in their abilities and honor their work. When giving feedback, tailor your teaching to each student's needs and sensibilities.

IN APPRECIATION OF BAD WRITING

I often get asked (privately) by members of my classes, "How can you always find something positive to say about every draft?" Sometimes I suspect that they think I am a Pollyanna or just faking my enthusiasm, but the truth is, I really do see something worthwhile about every submission, with or without narrative occasion.

My workshop has only two prerequisites: you have to be willing to write; and you have to be willing to revise. Given this open-door policy, we have seen group members who struggle to eke out a two-page submission alongside others who turn over every rock in their stream-of-consciousness. We have seen stories without any story, four essays packed into one, endings that ought to be beginnings, and flashbacks piled on flashbacks. We have waded through deep-purple prose, dodged countless eyes roaming around the room, and have tried to envision how a character could be "walking on thin ice" while "spinning his wheels." If adverbs were currency, some of the writing in my workshops could save Social Security.

It's not that I don't recognize all this bad writing when I read it. But part of the reason it doesn't dampen my enthusiasm is because I don't see bad writing as bad. I see it as part of the creative process. In fact, I think it is pretty safe to say that if it weren't for bad writing, there wouldn't be much good writing, because literature doesn't just burst forth fully armed, like Athena from Zeus's head. As writers, we are the accumulation of all the writing we have done in our lives. We learn from writing things that work, and we learn just as much from writing things that don't work. So in this sense, even bad writing is good. Every draft is a success in that it paves the way for the ones that will follow, and follow, and follow.

Yet when we are providing feedback on a work-in-progress, most of us tend to lose sight of how the creative process works, and how good writing *evolves* through an accumulation of drafts. We look at a writer's nascent efforts, and we make snap judgments about her abilities and think snooty comments—*Why did she even bother to submit something so bad?* We see a lack of narrative techniques and use those deficits as a strike against the writer. *What a waste of our reading time,* we think, when in fact the reality is exactly the opposite. As feedback providers and writers, we need to remember that it is from four hundred pages of imperfect drafts that the best two-hundred-page books emerge. If we must use the term "bad writing," then we must also acknowledge this: bad writing is what germinates good writing.

A while back, two new participants joined my workshop at the same time. One had wanted to try writing a personal narrative for years, but even though she was bold enough to serve as chair of her community's school board, she couldn't muster the courage to give it a try. Then she turned forty and realized that she was even more afraid of going through her whole life *without* trying to write her memoir because that wasn't the kind of person she wanted to be. The other new participant came to the workshop with an MFA and had written a novel way back when, which didn't get published (not enough plot, apparently). So he traded in that failure for a respectable job and family and didn't write another word of fiction for fifteen years, until a mutual friend gently bullied him into taking my workshop.

When the session started, the chair of the school board volunteered to have her pages critiqued first, just so she wouldn't chicken out. And the MFA fellow with the unpublished manuscript set himself a goal of one thousand words a day. Do you think when I read that school-board chair's first eight pages full of honest emotion that I saw her clumsy point-of-view shifts as reason for discouragement? Do you think when I read the opening chapters of the MFA graduate's long-delayed second novel that his occasional authorial intrusions really mattered in writing that hinted at phenomenal talent? Just look at what these two people had already achieved! They were writing! They were writing! They were on their way! What's not to appreciate, except a blank page?

But seeing someone try creative writing for the first time, and come back to it after a setback, aren't the only reasons I appreciate all the writing in my workshop. Let me tell you about my "regulars." Some of these writers have been in my classes off and on for years, before I had children and crow's-feet, before I had written any books on writing or my essay collections. After all these years together, my regulars know all about my bossy tendencies, my belief in the miracle of revision, and my narrative pet peeves (a single tear, introductory clauses, the word "tiny"). And I know all about this one's bad habit of run-on sentences, and that one's difficultly with internal monologue, and how this fellow writes beautifully but struggles with such debilitating self-doubt he can't seem to finish his almost-finished memoir.

I credit my regulars for helping me truly understand the creative process. Draft after draft, story after story, year after year, they have shown me how you have to start *somewhere* or you will never start, how order emerges from chaos, and how powerful stories come from humble beginnings. Recently, we critiqued one of the last chapters of a novel that had started a couple years ago from a fifteen-minute, in-class writing exercise. Witnessing this participant's progress every step of the way—the trials and errors as she developed her characters and discovered her plot and revised or tweaked everything from the structure to the dialogue tags—taught me as much about writing as a hundred books on craft. Now the novel is down to the polishing stage and shows such promise it recently earned her a generous grant from a writing foundation.

I am grateful for this privilege I have been given to bear witness to stories, real and imagined, in the making. I love the opportunity to talk about the craft of writing, and then to see how the feedback is processed and put into practice. And I love every writer in my workshops. Even if I don't love them in real life, I love them when their stories are being discussed. Here they are, taking emotional risks and exposing their work to criticism when they could be home safe, reading a good book. They have entrusted me and the other members of the workshop to read their work in the hopes we can help them make it better.

This isn't just an act of courage, but generosity. Writers need to see other writers in the thick of it. We need to see the creative process at work. Otherwise—just like the school-board chair who was afraid to try creative writing—we too could find ourselves avoiding the blank page for fear that what might come out is *bad writing!* We could find ourselves feeling discouraged about our own disastrous drafts to the point of quitting. Whenever I feel this way at my own writing desk, I remember all the "bad" writing in my workshops, and it cheers me up. Not because these people failed, but because, ultimately, they succeeded. And if they can succeed by persevering, then maybe, just maybe, so can I. And so I keep writing.

In exchange for the writer's generosity, feedback providers need to make a point of putting bad writing in perspective. Bad writing is what it is—here today, likely gone in another few drafts, and likely to return at the start of a new story, or poem, or chapter. By acknowledging—even appreciating—the role of bad writing in the creative process, we can stop using it as a judgment against the writer, or treating it as the eight-hundred-pound elephant in the room that everyone sees but no one dares to mention. And once you put bad writing in perspective, it is easy to look past the problems in any piece of writing and see its potential.

In a previous chapter, I mentioned that my writing workshop used to meet in a seldom-used back room of my former house. Sometimes when I was there alone, struggling in the midst of my own bad writing, I would wander back to that room in the quiet of midweek. There was our haphazard circle of vacant, green plastic chairs, and the stain on the pink rug where my dog had a long-ago accident, and a column of dust particles illuminated in a sunbeam. I saw all of those imperfections, but I also saw so much more.

That room was alive with ten years' worth of characters sharing their stories. I saw a fiddle-playing detective who solved a grisly crime, a fisherman's wife who left her husband after he gambled away their life savings, and a teenage zombie who just wanted to be loved. I saw an Iraq war veteran who found peace in his calling as a coach, bug-like aliens that took over the earth, and a middle-aged woman who finally found the wherewithal to confront the demons from her past. I saw an engineer at Los Alamos who altered history by stopping the development of the A-Bomb, an old-time logger who searched a lifetime for a mythical tree, and a little girl rocking back and forth against the wall outside her parent's bedroom as she waited for her cancer-stricken mother to die.

This is what comes from bad writing. This is potential fulfilled, scenes that transport me; writing so good I feel humbled to know the writer; finished short stories, memoirs, essays, and novels rich in life, drama, entertainment, and meaning. And I was there! I got to witness their creation and watch them develop from nothing to really something.

Somebody asks, "How can you always find something good to say about every submission?" My answer—"How can you not? Just step into that back room and see what I see."

Feedback and the Real World

The following was a small but significant scene from back when I was married.

I hurried out the front door, late for meeting a friend for coffee at the bookstore. I stepped outside to find that the car was gone, or at least the only car I could drive because our other rust bucket was a standard, and I never was able to learn how to shift and accelerate at the same time, not with so many important things on my mind. My husband must have taken my car to drive our daughters to the movies. Who knew when he would be back, given that the man never ran out of errands?

Naturally, I was put out by this inconvenience, especially since I'd let him know that morning that I was going out later to meet my friend. When my husband eventually moseyed on home, I reminded him of our conversation. "We even talked about my meeting," I said. "Remember, I told you I'd stop by the bank because I'd be right next door, *meeting my friend at the bookstore.*"

"We didn't talk about it," my husband replied. "You told me you were going out, and I didn't pay attention."

Breakdowns in communication happen all the time. Here, I am not talking about within the writing realm, but in the real world at large. Just pick up any newspaper and read the screaming headlines, or look at the evidence closer to home: town meetings that dissolve into shouting matches between neighbors, church groups and PTA committees that suffer under the tyranny of one or two members, couples that break up because one partner is miserable while the other one thinks everything is happily ever after. The workplace, too, is fraught with bad communication. A program director for a three-day conference once told me about the time she landed a much-coveted keynoter. When she emailed this exciting news to her coworker, along with a quick FYI that the conference center's pool would be closed for repairs, the only response from her coworker was, "Oh, that's too bad, I like to swim." Another friend who works in marketing communications once told me that her boss had written on her employee evaluation that she was "stupid." *Stupid.* How does that improve job performance? And how did this boss rise to the top of a field with the word *communication* in its descriptor?

This book focuses on feedback and writing, but most of the issues addressed in these pages are just as applicable to *any* kind of communication between people. After all, feedback is just that—a form of communication, one that permeates our daily lives. Whether you are helping your child with their homework, or brainstorming a new product idea at a business meeting, or asking the waiter to take back your overcooked steak, you are giving or receiving feedback.

Consider the tiff I had with my now-former husband after he left me stranded at home without a car. "*You told me you were going out, and I didn't pay attention.*" It is tempting to leave you with that comment, and with the impression that I was blameless in this situation, but that would mean omitting a few key details. For example, when I told my husband I was going out later that day, I was heading up the kitchen stairs at the time, too busy to wait for his response. I also was feeling guilty for assuming he would be available to watch the kids, and I know my tone reflected my defensiveness. In one of the previous chapters, I emphasize that it is not just what you say, but how you say it and when you say it that can make all the difference between being heard and being obnoxious. From this, you can draw your own conclusions.

My hope with this book is that you and I both use these insights about feedback to enrich not only our writing, but our relationships and our work lives as well. When we are aware of the emotional factors underlying our interactions with family, friends, and coworkers, we can communicate with more sensitivity and clarity. When we are open to other people's perspectives, we will discover new opportunities to learn and to grow. When we remain true to our own instincts, we can change for the better and never feel compromised. When we show faith in people and treat them with respect, we are much more likely to gain the ear and the respect of others. When we are positive in our words and in our attitude, life will be easier, even when it is hard. And when we make a conscious effort to connect with others, even at the risk of exposing ourselves to judgment, we will be contributing to a collective goodwill that can change the world.

Way back when, I started jotting down notes for a book about feedback, but then children, a few other book ideas, and a wee bit of procrastination intervened. All that time, however, my enthusiasm for the idea never waned. I knew just what I wanted to say about feedback, if I only had the chance to put these thoughts and feelings into a book. Then I got the chance. My friend and former editor, John Landrigan, invited me to submit a proposal for *Toxic Feedback*. For this small gesture of encouragement—which made a huge difference—I remain truly appreciative.

I am equally appreciative to my current editor, Elise McHugh, and all the talented folks at the University of New Mexico Press for giving me this opportunity to revise and expand *Toxic Feedback* in this second edition. If I may offer a bit of unsolicited feedback: You guys are the best!

Toxic Feedback is derived from my own experiences as a feedback receiver and provider and from my educational conversations with hundreds of aspiring and published authors, writing group participants, creative-writing teachers, professional editors, and friends. So many people were willing to share with me their knowledge and stories related to this subject. Without their generosity—and especially their feedback—this book would not have been possible.

For saying "yes" to an interview and making my day, many thanks to Samina Ali, Jennifer Crusie, Ernest Hebert, Khaled Hosseini, Don Johnson, Ted Kooser, Patrick Madden, Archer Mayor, Gregory Maguire, Juan Morales, Grace Paley, Jodi Picoult, Matthew Salesses, Sarah Stewart Taylor, and Crystal Wilkinson.

And to the most nontoxic person I know, much love to Helmut Baer, my partner in life and creative adventures.

Joni B. Cole teaches creative writing online and at her own Writer's Center in White River Junction, Vermont. She is also an independent workshop facilitator at Dartmouth College and a frequent teacher and speaker at academic programs, conferences, libraries, and social-service organizations across the country. Cole is the author of seven books, including *Good Naked: How to Write More, Write Better, and Be Happier* (listed as one of the "best books for writers" by *Poets & Writers* magazine). She is also a contributor to *The Writer* magazine and the author of the essay collection *Party Like It's 2044: Finding the Funny in Life and Death*. For more information, visit jonibcole.com.